D1280186

ONE RETURNED

by

Robert R. "Bob" Twitchell

I DEDICATE THIS BOOK

TO

MRS. OLIVIA M. TWITCHELL

MY MOTHER

The last chapter, titled "Lest We Forget," is dedicated in memory of the late United States Senator "HENRY M. JACKSON."

This tribute is in appreciation of Senator Henry M. Jackson's sincerity, diligence and able assistance in completing an otherwise unattainable goal.

"He cared."

"ONE RETURNED"

"The saga of a WWII United States Marine veteran who returned 36 years later to the battlegrounds where he had fought and was twice wounded. His mission — to exorcise the ghosts of a lifetime — confronts the reader with history at a personal level and an opportunity to experience the unique cultures of the Central Pacific."

By
Robert R. "Bob" Twitchell

THE WAR IN THE PACIFIC 1941-45

1941:	Dec. 7	Japan launches attacks against Pearl Harbor, Guam, Wake, Midway, Hong Kong, Malaysia and the Philippines. (Date is Dec. 8 west of International Date Line.)
	Dec. 23	Wake Island surrenders as U.S. rescue effort stalls.
	Dec. 25	British surrender Hong Kong.
1942:	Jan. 3	Army strategists in Washington say aid to troops in Philippines would be "unjustifiable diversion" from "principal" theater — the Atlantic."
	Mar. 11	As ordered by Roosevelt, Gen. Douglas MacArthur leaves Corregidor.
	Mar. 21	First Americans of Japanese ancestry arrive at Manzanar camp in California.
	Apr. 9	Surrender of Bataan.
	Apr. 18	Sixteen B-25s commanded by Lt. Col. James Doolittle bomb five Japanese cities. Inflict little damage but boost U.S. morale.
	May 4-8	Battle of Coral Sea. First naval battle by ships which cannot see one another. U.S. losses include carrier Lexington. Japanese lose small carrier Shoho.
	May 6	Corregidor falls.
	June 3-6	Battle of Midway. U.S. losses: carrier Yorktown, destroyer, 147 planes. Japanese losses: four carriers, heavy cruiser, 322 planes. Turning point in Pacific war.
	Aug. 7	Marines land on Guadalcanal and satellite islands. First U.S. offensive.

	Aug. 8-9	Battle of Savo island. U.S., Australia lose 1,023 men, four cruisers against Japanese loss of 58 men.
	Aug. 9	U.S. ships withdraw from Guadalcanal with 2,000 unlanded troops and half of Marines 60-day food supply.
	Aug. 12	Marines land on Espiritu Santo in Solomons.
	Aug. 17	U.S. wipes out garrison on Makin Island, forcing Japanese to heavily fortify nearby Tarawa.
	Sept. 12-14	After losing 1,200 men, Japanese give up attempt to take Guadalcanal's Bloody Ridge.
	Oct. 11-12	Battle of Cape Esperance. Japanese cruiser, three destroyers sunk. U.S. loses destroyer.
	Oct. 14	Japanese destroy 48 of 90 planes on Henderson Field.
	Nov. 12-16	Naval Battle of Guadalcanal. U.S. loses four destroyers, two light cruisers. Dead include five sons of Mr. and Mrs. Thomas Sullivan of Iowa. Japanese lose two battleships, heavy cruiser.
	Nov. 15	2,000 Japanese killed attempting to land on Guadalcanal.
1943:	Feb. 8	U.S. secures Guadalcanal at loss of 1,490 lives. About 23,000 Japanese lives lost, but 13,000 troops are evacuated safely.
	Oct. 31	Marines land on Bougainville.
	Nov. 20	Marines invade Tarawa, capture it in 76 hours at cost of more than 1,000 lives. Of 4,500 Japanese, only 17 are taken prisoner.
1944:	Jan. 31	U.S. invades Kwajalein, world's largest atoll, taking it in five days.

Feb. 17	Army and Marines invade Eniwetok. Secured it Feb. 22.
June 15	Marines invade Saipan, followed by Army. Fighting ends July 9. Approximate losses: 3,000 Americans, 50,000 Japanese.
June 18	Hideki Tojo resigns as Japan's premier.
June 19	U.S. destroys 346 Japanese planes while losing only 30 in air battle portion of the Battle of the Philippine Sea. It becomes known as the Great Marianas Turkey Shoot.
July 21	Marines and Army land on Guam, find welcome sign left by Navy frogmen. Guam captured after two weeks of heavy resistance. 1,500 Americans, 3,500 Japanese killed.
July 24	U.S. invades Tinian island, from which planes carrying atomic bombs will take off, is captured in nine days.
Sept. 15	Marines, Army, invade Peleleiu. Fighting ends Nov. 25. U.S. lose 1,794 men on island that is of no strategic value. Japanese loses about 10,000.
Dec. 29	Military advised that atomic bomb should be available for its use by August 1, 1945.
1945: Feb. 19	U.S. lands on Iwo Jima. Fighting continues into June at cost of 6,000 American lives, 25,000 wounded. Japanese losses: 20,000 killed.
Feb. 23	During second raising of U.S. flag on Iwo Jima's Mount Suribachi, photographer Joe Rosenthal takes the most famous photo of the Pacific War.
Mar. 9-10	Tokyo firebombed by 334 B-29s with loss of life estimated at about

		100,000. One million homeless.
	Apr. 1	60,000 U.S. troops land on Okinawa. Battle, which includes fierce Kamikaze attacks in surrounding waters, ends June 22. U.S. casualties: 7,373 killed, 31,807 wounded. Japanese: at least 107,539 killed, 10,755 captured. 75,000 civilian casualties.
	Apr. 12	Franklin Roosevelt dies.
	May 23-25	U.S. bombers lay waste to 16 square miles of Tokyo, but spare Imperial Palace of the Emperor.
	July 16	Dawn of Atomic Age. Bomb exploded at Alamorgordo, New Mexico.
	July 30	U.S. cruiser Indianapolis sunk with loss of 883 lives in largest U.S. single-ship disaster of the war.
	Aug. 6	Atomic bomb dropped on Hiroshima. Obliterates 10 square miles and takes 130,000 lives.
	Aug. 9	Atomic bomb dropped on Nagasaki. 35,000 killed. Center of city destroyed but damage limited because surrounding hills act as shield.
	Aug. 14	Japan surrenders
	Aug. 15	Bitter Japanese officers of Western Headquarters Command murder 16 U.S. prisoners of war.
	Aug. 18	Despite surrender, 14 Japanese fighters attack B-32s (only 15 of which saw combat) during photo-reconaissance mission over Japan.
	Sept. 2	Japanese sign surrender terms aboard USS Missouri.
1974:	Mar. 9	Hiroo Onoda, last known Japanese soldier of Pacific War, surrenders in Philippines.

TABLE OF CONTENTS

Page	Description of Pictures

All pictures were taken by the author unless otherwise noted.

AUTHOR'S NOTE

My book, "One Returned," is not meant to be a balanced story of the war with Japan. It is in no way a history lesson, nor do I intend it to be such.

Many books have been written over the years which accurately plot movements of the Army, Navy, and Marine Forces, I am not competing with them. This book was not written in chronological order, it is of my order, of thoughts and rememberences. I have tried however, to chart in an orderly manner as possible a venture for you into the realms of a struggle for life and the facing of death, of a United States Marine in World War II.

I am presenting it to you after 36 years of being hidden in the darkness of my memory. Much technical data which I wasn't privileged to at the time, nor did I then much care about has been supplied through various histories of the battles.

Accuracy is most important to me and I have worked hard to bring you a story as accurate as anyone can relate after the passing of almost a lifetime.

Guadalcanal was my first indoctrination to battle, it was there I faced the wily enemy in the jungles and caves, night and day. During three months of living on field rations and hope, we drove the enemy back into the jungles with little more than guts and the name, "Marine," to keep us going. Early in 1943 I was evacuated to New Zealand to recover from Malaria, Yellow Jaundice and Dysentery, diseases common in the tropics. My next bout with the enemy came nine months later on the bloody beaches of "Tarawa," the first assault wave in an amphibous tractor along the pier, "Red Beach 2." On that first day, November 20, 1943, I became one of the many fighting casualties. It was no time to stop and no place to go but forward to secure the badly needed airstrip. On these beaches I earned my first Purple Heart, along with many of my comrades, completing an entire 76 hours of fighting with shrapnel in my arm and hand.

In my last campaign against the Japanese, "Saipan," I was shot in the right leg, another Purple Heart. I was unable to go further. My discharge read, "Honorable, Medical, Gunshot wound right leg and Malaria."

My story is a remembrance of events that have haunted me for these many years. By telling it I was able to at last excorcise the ghosts that had occupied my mind and body these past thirty-six years.

I dedicate this book to my understanding and loving mother, who gave me the courage not only to fight a war but to return to its battlegrounds and take it on again.

MAPS

Books Used to Research Biography

"FOLLOW ME" — By Richard W. Johnston, Published by Random House 1948.

"TARAWA" — By Robert Sherrod, Published by Admiral Nimitz Foundation, Fredricksburg, Texas 1944, 1954, 1973.

"KIRIBATI, ASPECTS OF HISTORY" — Published for the occasion of the independence of Kiribati, 1979. Published by the Institute of Pacific Studies and Extension Services, University of South Pacific and the Minister of Education, Training and Culture, Kiribati Government.

"A PATTERN OF ISLANDS" — By Arthur Grimble, first published in 1952. Published in Great Britain by Cox and Wyman Ltd. London. Published by John Murry Ltd.

Cover Design by Trace Swann

PROLOGUE

Trained fighting Marines were badly needed during those early days of the war with the Japanese as replacements for Marines killed, wounded, or down with tropical diseases. That was the condition during "Boot Camp" with no leaves or furloughs as were allowed during peacetime. We were permitted several liberties to the big city of Los Angeles. It was a great town but not much to howl about. Hell, we were still just kids with shaved heads. How soon that would change!

What is the make-up of a United States Marine? That question was always a puzzle to me, that is until I served with the "Corps" in three major battles. Now I can say with authority — a Marine is only a boy sent to do a man's job — and he does it. He is told he is the best, receives tough and factual training — adapting to all situations very quickly — or he is sent home in a box, or lay buried among the coral sands through the ages of time.

It is the "Esprit de Corps" that drives a United States Marine through battle. It is a Marine's sense of honor, his courage and youth combined with the ability to take orders and carry these orders out under all kinds of conditions. That is my definition of a United States Marine.

Often I have been asked, Why did I choose to enlist in the United States Marine Corps? It wasn't that I was close to being drafted, and certainly never saw myself as overly brave. Just an average American boy who dropped out of high school in my senior year, (which I made up while in the service and for which I received my diploma), to work in the Boeing Airplane defense plant in Seattle, Washington.

Ask anyone over 50 years of age, where he or she was on December 7, 1941, and I am sure they could tell you without hesitation. On that Sunday I was working in a service station on the outskirts of Everett, Washington, pumping gas and doing minor mechanical work. Had you asked me where Hawaii was located at that time, I would have had to guess it was some far off foreign land, it was beyond comprehension — so far away.

A few days later at the local theatre the newsreels showed the graphic pictures of the bombing of Pearl Harbor. Shortly before, we had received a letter from my brother, who was com-

1

The Author, Robert R. "Bob" Twitchell, pictured after graduation from United States Marine Boot camp in 1942, within two weeks of this photo he was aboard ship for his first indocturnation to battle, "Guadalcanal."

manding officer of a destroyer escort, stationed at Pearl Harbor. Now, watching the destruction on the newsreels, I may have been witnessing his ship being blown apart. Hawaii was not very far away anymore.

December 8, 1942, I quit the service station and was hired

on at Boeing Aircraft Co. to work in the Anodizing department. It was without a doubt the dirtiest job in the entire plant. I would fill Boeing B-17 motor mounts with hot linseed oil, then turn them upside down to drain. The mounts were then taken to the Electro-flux department, tested for weak welds, then returned to me to clean up before going to the paint shop.

I always smelled of the oil, and I felt dirty and undesirable. While I was contributing to the war effort — it wasn't enough. In July 1942, with my mother, who had to sign for me, I drove to Seattle, Washington to enlist. My reason for choosing the Marine Corps — sounds a bit silly now, but I had always looked upon myself as an ugly duckling and was told you had to be nice looking as well as physically fit to be accepted in the Marine Corps. I felt it was a challenge — and I was accepted. I was a Marine and I was proud.

Upon arrival at boot camp, "Recruit Depot" in San Diego I soon realized looks had nothing to do with being accepted or rejected. I believe my drill sergeant was about the ugliest man I had ever seen — we didn't need a bulldog for a mascot, we had one — "the drill sergeant."

I was also soon to learn being a recruit Marine was about the lowest form of life on the face of the earth. Everyone ranked above you, you were required to salute everyone and everything, called anybody who walked "sir," ran to all formations and were told you would learn to love every bit of it.

Halfway through boot camp, a couple of days before going to the rifle range, the newspapers shouted through their big black banners, "MARINES LANDING ON GUADALCANAL." This was an island I have to admit not one person in the platoon had ever heard of.

We soon found out it was in the "Solomon group," which as far as any of us knew could be on the other side of the earth — it was! Each day the newspapers reported on a new battle being fought. Our comrades were upholding the tradition of the corps. We all cheered upon reading and listening to the accounts of the battles making new history for the United States Marine Corps, it was "Gung Ho—Let's Go." Little did any of us recruits realize that in just a few short weeks we would be fighting, side-by-side with those heroes we had been reading about.

Many inspections and much letter writing took place just before we were to board ship. To where, we had no idea. Just before loading we were issued a complete new issue of khaki,

The Author, Robert "Bob" Twitchell pictured after fighting on Guadalcanal, Tarawa and Saipan, 1945.

field greens and, oh yes, mosquito netting. It was obvious we were not going to Iceland.

The S.S. Tryon, a new liberty ship, was to be our home for the next few weeks and was it ever packed with bodies, live ones. We were offered three meals a day, but to take advantage of those three meals, it was necessary to stand in line constantly, a line that curled around the deck of the ship several times.

No sooner would the breakfast line be through than a lunch line started. Then supper. Lines, lines, lines! Bunks were in short supply, so many of us took turns to make the best use of them. Many men slept topside, and others took turns in a card game that went on 24 hours a day. There was even a line for the use of the head (bathroom).

Our first stop was Honolulu where we were granted a kind of liberty. More of rest and relaxation. Like a beer bust on the sandy beach. I made an attempt to locate my brother who commanded the destroyer escort based there, but had no luck.

Our next stop was in the New Hebredes where we pulled in for supplies. It was there we saw our first evidence that a war was being fought. The harbor was filled with ships, many of which suffered heavy damage from enemy guns and torpedoes. We were beginning to feel farther from home and closer to hell.

Leaving New Hebredes it became obvious we were not traveling a direct route. Watching the wake of our ship we could witness the zig-zagging pattern we were leaving in the Blue Pacific. This zig-zagging, frequent abandon ship drills and wild semaphoring between ships, along with intermittent gun practice, made us well aware we were in dangerous waters. Just a couple of days before sighting the "Canal" more naval escorts and several more transports joined us.

After a hearty breakfast of beans and cold cuts, we made preparations to disembark on Guadalcanal to serve as replacements for the front line fighting. During the preparations all hell broke loose overhead. The sky filled with black puffs of anti-aircraft fire. Every gun available on deck of all naval and transport ships began firing almost at once. Coming in, in an attempt to destroy us before we could even get on land, were twenty-eight Japanese torpedo planes out of the west. Thank God none were able to penetrate due to the able marksmanship of Naval, Coast Guard and Marine gunners. All were shot down before reaching their target.

That day, one of the longest I can ever remember, was just beginning as we went ashore on Guadalcanal amid mountains of rations, ammunition and communications equipment.

I had a pack filled with clean underwear, socks and a new set of khakis. Everyone had taken showers the night before, but soon we were to be raggedy-ass Marines and it would happen in just a few action-packed days.

Assignments were made for us to join different companies. In fact it took only a few minutes after landing. I was assigned to George (G) Company, 2nd Battalion, 2nd Regiment, 2nd Division, and my immediate family was to be the 3rd platoon and the 3rd squad. After hearing of the 3rd platoon's exploits and meeting the platoon leader, Lt. Logie, I felt honored to be a part of them. The C.O. Lt. Logie was a sergeant when he had left the States and was granted a field commission aboard ship. He was a born leader and a man who we all looked up to with a great deal of respect.

Being a fresh new Marine among Old Salts dressed in dirty and ragged clothes and wearing stubby beards, I soon gave them all my clothes I had carried ashore in my field pack. They looked so pathetic and dirty. Little did I realize soon I would look like them. We had been issued the new Gerand semi-automatic rifle and the old salts were still carrying the old 1903 bolt action Springfield 30-30. Several of the new replacements exchanged their newer rifles for the old. I didn't at that time but it wasn't long before I had inherited one of the old Springfield 30-30's, which I found to be much more dependable in that hot, wet, muddy terrain.

When I left the beach to join my new outfit I carried only my rifle, ammunition and the clothes on my back. I believed we were to be held in a staging or indoctrination center (a place where we would be given all the scoop). It was not to be, for in a couple of hours of landing I, along with many of my comrades, found ourselves on the front lines, with the enemy just a few yards away in the steaming jungle waiting for a chance to overrun our position and earn themselves a place in Shinto Heaven.

During the next three months it was charge, patrol, dig in, stand watch, play cards and pray. Not necessarily in that order. When the torrential rains came, which was almost every day, the mud generated was unbelievable. Up to your waist in the gooey stuff one minute and in a couple of hours it was so dry you could drive a jeep across it.

A boy quickly becomes a man in combat, and the boy who landed on Guadalcanal was soon to become that man. After several months of jungle living and fighting I was evacuated to New Zealand, suffering from Yellow Jaundice, Malaria and Dysentery.

Nine months later it was the "Battle of Tarawa," a 76 hour

6

war within a war. It was there I received my first Purple Heart award for wounds received in action. Seven months after the "Battle of Tarawa" I was a participant in the beach-head and fighting on "Saipan" in the Marianas. It was on Saipan I was awarded a second Purple Heart, for gunshot wound to my right leg. It was necessary for evacuation to Guadalcanal for treatment. After a too short hospital stay I was returned to full duty on Saipan where I continued on patrols until the infection from my leg would become too much for the tropical area and I was returned to the United States.

In writing this book of remembrances I hope to tell it like it was from the eyes of the enlisted man. Telling what I feel is important and also including some incidents that never really mattered except to the person it happened to, from my indoctrination to battle on the ridges of Guadalcanal, to the blood letting on Betio, Tarawa Atoll, and ending on the cave infested island of Saipan where I earned my second Purple Heart.

Today, nearly a lifetime later, with the passing of over 37 years, I am returning to those haunting beaches which have lived in my mind day and night reminding me of my promise.

During those 37 years I have led an active life and gathered many rewards — the raising of three healthy children into adulthood made me a proud parent. Serving my community as Chief of Police, then twice elected the post of County Sheriff after which I was elected and served as county freeholder, (helping write a charter for a new form of county government) made me a sensitive and informed public servant. With all my active life, private and personal, never once did I forget my time of service with those brave young Marines thousands of miles from home, in battles fought with fervor and winner take all.

In writing this book I wanted the reader to become closer to feeling the experiences of a "Young Marine growing up fast," and an insight into the comaraderie he and his "buddies" shared during those dark days of World War II.

The author, Robert "Bob" Twitchell pictured in 1955 upon his election as Snohomish County Sheriff. He was the youngest sheriff ever elected in the State of Washington.

8

CHAPTER I

A FLIGHT INTO THE PAST

"What in hell am I doing here?" I ask myself as I sat on the runway aboard Continental Airlines flight #86 waiting to take off from the Seattle-Tacoma airport this ninth day of December, 1979. "What brought me here?" I ask myself over and over. "When was my final decision to return to the past made?" After all it had been over thirty seven years since that day in 1942 when I left the United States as a young Marine to make the world a safe place in which to live, a world I knew nothing about and, I may add, still know very little of.

My conscious and subconscious thoughts keep returning to those faraway days when, upon returning to the United States, I vowed someday I would return. Not like General Douglas McArthur, with a fanfare and newsreel cameras grinding (at that time T.V. was not in production) but I would return in reverence as tribute to the memories of those who died so the rest of us may live in the freedom we have always enjoyed. I am close to that reality. In but a few minutes I will be airborne on the first leg of my "flight into the past." I feel confident many others made that vow, the same as I. I am proud that "I, for one, returned."

Traveling light, with my camera bag loaded with camera and plenty of film, a small suitcase that barely fits under my airplane seat, and a garment bag which holds several pairs of trousers and a sport coat which I was able to hang in the middle of the plane. I was certain my worries were over as for misplaced or lost luggage. I was to learn as my trip progressed that even the small amount of luggage I chose to take with me would be more than enough and, as I gathered souvenirs on my journey, I left behind some of the clothing in order to make room. I haven't heard of any coldsnap in the tropics, but if one should occur I know a couple of natives who will be well-prepared.

On the runway of the SeaTac Airport, Seattle, Washington, the huge DC 10 strained — then moved forward seemingly eager as I was to begin the journey that would take me into the past.

Flying over the Pacific Ocean, with my nose pressed tightly against the glass window, I could catch glimpses through wisps of clouds, of the water thousands of feet below, carrying logs and debris back and forth with the tides. I thought to myself what an effective advertisement a picture of this sight would make to promote ecology. Who would ever believe our oceans are so polluted thousands of miles from land?

The first stop: the Islands of Hawaii, and in particular the island of Oahu. I close my eyes in thought as we make the approach for our landing and remember, thirty five years ago, thousands and thousands of servicemen, coming and going. There were long lines at the bars, long lines at the restaurants and even longer lines at the brothels which were located just over a small bridge which ran along a creek or small river. Memories are dim but I have a memory locked away in my mind of waiting in a long line (I was only 19) and, as yet, had not tasted the joys of sex.

The nearest I ever got to sex up to then, was back in Everett (my home town). I smile to myself as I think of how daring I thought it to be when I sneaked my hand under a sweater and felt of my date's naked breast. The time was never right, nor did the place we happened to be seem safe enough. Now I felt, "Hell, I am still a virgin and a United States Marine." This was the time even if I had to pay for it.

After waiting in line for what seemed like hours, I'm sure it was, I finally had reached the top of the stairs, a place where I could see the girls in all their glory, strutting and prancing from room to room with just a towel hanging loosely in front of them. I felt the feelings that all men must feel when aroused — I couldn't wait.

From this vantage point, at the top of the stairs, it was easy to figure out the system. There were five girls, if you could call them girls. They all appeared to be twice my age, a tender nineteen. Each girl had two small rooms or cubicles where she conducted her business. There was a space in each room for only a bed and a night stand. A man (or boy about to become a man) would enter a room, undress. Soon a lady would enter, examine him, wash his privates, give him about two minutes of squealing delight and then she would leave him to dress quickly for another was waiting to take his place. In the meantime, she was entering her second room as assigned to her, to take care of one more. What a production line! The girls would make a round trip every five or six minutes.

One of the girls stopped almost directly in front of me, wiped her forehead and said to the lady in charge, "Ma, I am not feeling too good. Just give me another twenty and let me have the rest of the day off." I was shocked. Not at my being there but at the callousness being displayed. Getting a sick feeling in the pit of my stomach, I turned and walked back down the stairs not even asking for my three dollars back which I had given the woman called Ma. I would wait, I decided, until the time and place were right to give up my virginity.

The second visit, equally strong in my memory of Hawaii, was on my return from having fought on Guadalcanal, Tarawa and Saipan. It was a stopover for the return to the States. My main interest was food, good food. I stopped at a restaurant, ordered from the menu: steak, two eggs, a large glass of milk and fresh lettuce. Oh, yes, I believe toast and a vegetable came with it. After this delicious meal, I sat for about twenty minutes waiting for my check which didn't arrive. The waitress who was waiting on me kept passing me by. By the way, she was a young Japanese girl as are many in Hawaii.

I finally caught her and asked her if I could *please* have my check to which she replied almost nonchalantly, "Jam your finger up your _____s." I, at first, felt hostile and said, "What did you say?" She then said, "Hey, Marine, I'm sorry. I'm so busy all the time. I didn't think. Please don't be mad. You're not mad are you?" I said, "No, I'm not mad." By this time I could imagine all the fresh guys punching and pulling, all that she had to take with her nationality not being of any help. She again asked, "You're sure you're not mad?" I again said no. She said three or four times, "Sure you're not mad?" to which I replied each time, "No." She then, with a look of scorn, said, "Then jam the other four up there."

I had just returned from fighting the Japanese and I must have seen red. I could see the sneaky Jap coming out of the jungle with his hands raised in surrender with another behind him. Then, close to our lines, the first Jap dropped to his knees. A nambu machine gun which was strapped to his back was then put into action by the Jap behind him. Also I had a severe gunshot wound in my right leg and it was difficult for me to walk even with a crutch as it was something I was not used to and the tropics had dealt the wound a set-back by causing a bad

11

infection but, with no trouble and without the crutch, I stood up and gave the waitress a straight jab with a fist in her face. She went end over end and all I remember was a lot of confusion and getting out of there and back to the base hospital where I never left again until I was loaded aboard ship for the return to the United States.

Now, thirty five years later, I am back. It is a new and exciting place, but I am not interested in this part of the past. It was then and is now, only a stopover and holds no real clue to what I endured those many years ago.

An hour before leaving Hawaii, one of the lenses fell from the frame of my glasses. The frame had broken right next to the nose piece; a difficult place to repair. There was no place in the short time I had on Oahu to get it mended so I did the next best thing; I found a tube of instant glue with which I managed to do a patch job. All through the trip, about every two days, it would break apart and I would patch it together again.

By the time I had arrived on the Tarawa atoll, I had used so much glue in patching that I had fastened the glass lens to the plastic frame. In so doing I had also smeared the lenses with so much instant glue it was nearly impossible to see with any clarity.

I had heard acetone would cut through the glue and permit it's removal, but where, oh where, could I find any acetone? Knowing fingernail polish remover contains acetone, I made inquiries with no success. Dillis, a New Zealander who worked in Betio for the United Nations, was the only white woman at the hotel and she was no help. She told me she never used any nail polish, or cosmetics of any kind, for that matter. After several more days of frantic searching, and my glasses becoming more and more useless, I was visited by Mrs. Dunnegan, an English woman, and the wife of the Minister of Education for the King George School. She offered no direct help but told me the wife of one of the teachers, a French girl, may know where I could find some nail polish remover. The next day I had the pleasure of meeting the darling French wife of the English teacher and I was overjoyed when she said she remembered seeing some bottles of fingernail polish remover in a small shop along the road to the Betio ferry landing.

I may state lots of shops are on the paths with not much for sale, but are a gathering place. When you live in the type of atmosphere that abounds Tarawa, a slow-hot-nobody-moves-much place you need lots of storage places.

The school bus that was taking me to the ferry stopped at the shop where I was told the fingernail polish remover was for sale. I entered the shop, no doors or windows; just a smiling shopkeeper and shelves of fish, crackers and miscellaneous. I asked for fingernail polish remover; no one understood. I spent ten minutes looking. Then the cute French girl came in and pointed to a row of bottles which was what I had been seeking. I asked the shopkeeper how much. She shrugged her shoulders, turned to a man who shrugged his shoulders and then they brought out lists (an inventory, I would suspect). They came to several pages, yellowing with age, and came upon the fingernail polish remover. It would cost me eighty five cents, which she said with a quizzical look, like maybe I wouldn't pay that much. I gladly exchanged money for this badly needed product which I would imagine had been on the shelf for a long time. There had been an even dozen bottles. Now there were eleven. I left with the thought that it must have been some pretty good salesman that came through selling fingernail polish remover a few years ago.

My trip was originally routed from Oahu to Majuro, then to the Tarawa atoll but a tidal wave had engulfed the tiny island of Majuro making it a health hazard to stay there and I would have had to stay there for several days waiting for the plane to Tarawa. I am re-routed to Johnson Island, "The last place Amelia Earhart was heard from on her ill-fated flight many years ago." I feel a sense of awe as we set down on the wind and rain swept runway. We are allowed off for just a few minutes. Only later I am to learn this island is a storage place for poison gas by the United States and getting off the plane is usually a "no no." We can see the primitive airport with, I would guess, every native on the island turning out to welcome their only contact with the outside world. It is as if we have landed on another planet.

Soon we are airborne and our next stop is Majuro which we are told will be a short visit. We are able to see huge tents erected by the Seabees for those made homeless just a few days earlier due to the damage by the tidal wave. We are told eight thousand out of the eleven thousand inhabitants on this island lost their homes but God was good to them as I learn only three of the eleven thousand are missing. After about forty five minutes we are airborne again.

We take on our plane from Majuro as many homeless natives as will fill the empty seats for evacuation to other islands. A young mother and her small son whom she is holding in her arms, share my seat. Neither the mother or I speak a language understandable to each other but smiles are universal and, knowing small children all like candy and remembering a chocolate bar I bought on Oahu, I bring it out of my pack. Showing it to the mother, I use sign language asking if I can give the bar to her son. Both seem happy about the offer and, with smiles, accept. It is only after unwrapping that I realize, with the heat, the chocolate bar has almost turned to hot chocolate and we all take turns going to the washroom in the rear of the plane to wash off this gooey mess.

Our next stop is to be Kwajalein in the Marshall Island group. It is just a small dot in the huge Pacific Ocean but carried a high profile in the early "Forties" as a rendevous for convoys enroute to islands in Japan's back yard. It was in 1944, just prior to the invasion of Saipan and Tinian in the Mariana group, we were setting just off shore waiting for the rest of the convoy to join us. One of the sailors aboard the transport had been fishing off the fantail and, using a hook made in the engine room and a hunk of pork, had hooked a shark which about six of us helped bring on deck. The shark was about eight feet long and a real nasty looking creature. One of the fellows mentioned getting the cook to cook it up and we all thought it a good idea. We sent word down to the galley and escorted one of the cooks topside telling him what a tasty morsel we had for him to prepare. The night was black as coal and no lights were allowed. The cook, a black man, was told where the fish was. He had come from a lighted area and his eyes were not accustomed to the dark so he felt around for the fish. Just as he put his hand on the shark it leaped banging hard on the deck. It was then the cook saw the size of the fish and it looked to him like he was going to be attacked. I really believe the cook turned white at that moment. He did an about face and ran, or I should say dove, down below mumbling as he left us, "I ain't going to do nothing with that monster."

It is as if a giant padlock has been removed from my memory and flooding forth are many nostaglic remembrances that have remained locked up for nearly forty years. When I first came home from the war, people used to say to me, "I'll bet you don't

14

want to talk aout it." So I, as well as many others, kept it all locked up. There were, however, many lighthearted moments worth talking about and remembering even when life seemed the darkest. One of these stories concerns the night just before the Battle of Saipan. This was to be my third assault on enemy beaches many miles from home and many others in the same position as I wondered what were the odds this time. What would the next morning bring?

One of the men in my squad had stolen, or I should say "liberated" a 30 cal. carbine belonging to one of the 2nd lieutenants. This gun was a much sought after prize by most of the naval officers aboard the transport. In trade, the carbine brought five bottles of hard liquor from a naval officer who asked no questions. One bottle of rum, one of brandy, and three of whisky. What a time and place to have a party! We all decided it was as good a time as any to get good and drunk. Hell, why not? Tomorrow we would all be dead anyway. How could anyone survive three landings and still come out of it alive? What were the odds? There were many more reasons to get drunk mentioned but those were enough.

The following morning after the "party," it must have been about 0400 or 4 a.m., I was rudely awakened by the ship's loudspeaker going, "BEEP!!! BEEP!!! BEEP!!! MAN YOUR BATTLE STATIONS. MAN YOUR BATTLE STATIONS." Coming in on the attack were Japanese planes and the sound from the ship's guns, "ACK . . . ACK . . . ACK . . . ACK" filled the air almost causing my head to explode. I became sick, real sick, throwing up all over myself. As I rolled around the cold steel deck, sick, with my clothes reeking of liquor that had tasted so good the night before and now recycled, I honestly prayed for the enemy bombs to hit me and end the misery, but alas, no luck.

In a short while which seemed like an eternity, the enemy planes were gone and I felt like I was really going to live and, by then, I actually wanted to. It was below decks for a salt water shower . . . all the fresh water was being used for the assault preparations . . . climb into clean clothes and join my squad on deck for the climb into the Higgens boats to head for the beach and another bout with death.

Shaking my head, I find I am not in a Higgens boat and it is 1979 and I am in an airplane which is still flled with refugees picked up on Majuro. Upon landing, these homeless but still smiling natives leave the plane to transfer for transportation to other islands where they will stay until their homes are restored or it is safe for them to return. We could learn a lot from these pople in caring and helping one another.

Soon we are again in the air and looking down. The island does not appear large enough for the landing of such a plane as we are aboard. Time goes fast and soon we are descending preparing for a landing on another small dot in the Pacific, an island called Ponape. Here I am to part with another of the many friends I made on this trip. He is a native of Ponape who attended and graduated from Oregon State University and is coming home to seek employment as a policeman even if, as he told me, a policeman is not much needed on Ponape.

Once again, as I often will be on this journey, I am lost in thoughts and remembrances. It was shortly after my discharge from the United States Marine Corps and between jobs. I held many — from selling advertising to managing a real estate office. An old Marine buddy of mine, "Moose" Larson, informed me of an opening in the town of Snohomish, Washington, for a policeman and, being the Chief of Police was a former Marine, only ex-Marines need apply.

I arrived in Snohomish about noon the next day where I met the Chief, "Charlie" Adams, who was making his rounds of the town. After introductions, he asked me when I could start. I said, "Any time." We walked around the city for about an hour while he introduced me to the merchants and told me which lights to turn off at 10 p.m. on Front Street.

Returning to the station, which was a small dingy room down three flights of stairs, I received a two hour indoctrination of the jail and office. Charlie Adams then pinned a badge on me, hung a 38 cal. Colt around my waist, put a hat on my head (which was a little small. My head, I mean) and said, "I'm going home. If you need me, call. The next shift comes on at midnight to relieve you." With that, I was the boss of the town, population thirty nine hundred, mostly loggers and good drinkers, but I soon found common sense, friendliness and to be stern when it was required, was all that you needed to get along.

So I began my work as an officer of the law as lowest on the list of a four-man police force in a town with eleven bars and about twice as many churches. Most of the laws that were broken had to do with drinking and fighting. Within three years

I had been promoted to the office of chief.

I was proud of my town and I guess the town was proud of me because when the election for sheriff of the county, the third larest county in the state, came up, several of the businessmen asked me to toss my hat in the ring. It was a large ring; the incumbent and seven other well-known lawmen. I managed to win handily and was re-elected four years later. Too bad the people I served weren't as law abiding as these wonderful, friendly, simple natives. As sheriff I was allowed only 21 deputies to handle the jail, civil department, criminal department, juvenile department, record room and dispatch center. In just a few short years of my leaving the office, the sheriff will be assigned over two hundred deputies and still that won't be enough. Being that the county is next door to the city of Seattle, it becomes a real challenge to keep it as crime-free as can possibly be done. I have always been proud of my record in eliminating and solving the crimes that occurred even if I had to do it in some unorthodox ways. That is another story to be told.

I consider myself fortunate in having seatmates on the entire trip who help to make the journey more bearable. The trip from Ponape to Guam is no exception. We land on the island of Guam in the Marianas at 4 a.m. What can a person do on Guam at four in the morning? I learn that Guam is to the Japanese what Hawaii is to the American tourist. Not wishing to part with fifty dollars for a hotel room for just a couple of hours, I decide to stay in the airport where I am to spend an enjoyable time talking with the many foreign travelers who are waiting to go in different directions.

Maybe it is the loss of sleep or the heat or just the closeness of one destination of my journey, but I am excited. The next stop is the island of Nauru and from Nauru I will board another plane for the ride to Tarawa. I find it difficult for me to keep an even keel. Tring to calm myself while waiting for the airplane to Nauru, I enter into conversations with many of the travelers who are also waiting for their planes to arrive. I had a few second thoughts about flying Nauru Airlines when a woman Japanese doctor, wearing thick glasses and having legs that would be a match for a crane, (her legs could, however, match mine quite well as I have about the skinniest legs on earth) talked with me. She told me many things about Nauru Airlines saying they were known in the area as the "relaxed airlines." The

17

The banker from Guadalcanal, "Nicholas Marovoy" (left) and "Wally" a native from Guadalcanal. The building in the background is the Naurau Hotel.

"Hotel Naurau," despite its modernistic look, still carries over some of the old traditions, i.e. nothing moves fast and service is almost unknown.

reason for this is that if a member of management or one of the pilots want to go to, say Hong Kong, for a party or to buy a gift or something else, they simply shut down the system and the passengers await their return by playing cards, visiting the bar, trying to keep cool or just visiting. A relaxed attitude is quite common in this part of the world.

Coming over Nauru was like landing in a fairyland, a small island about three square miles, it is quite an experience as was landing on most of the small islands in the huge Pacific Ocean. Nauru has one road which mainly goes from the airport to the hotel and each time a plane lands or takes off, the road is closed for use as an extra runway. Perhaps I should not say "extra," "necessary" would be more precise. The Nauru Airlines used Boeings 720's as did most of the airlines of the Pacific. There were no problems, however the pilots are used to the island landings and despite the seemingly casual operation policies all airline employees do their job in a professional manner.

Coming in I was sure we wouldn't have room to brake to a stop but as we passed a couple of cars I realized we were using the road to complete our landing. As we approached the terminal it is as if all the natives from each island are following us and waiting to greet our arrival as a large welcome or maybe they are just here for their own entertainment — like when I was a small child we used to line up along side the railroad tracks to wave at the engineer.

The stairway in the tail drops, we disembark and it is another trip through customs. It is always uncomfortable, here I believe it is even more so. We speak different languages and it is so darn hot. They don't know what an air conditioner is over here.

I spend some time just looking, then I inquire as best I can the way to the hotel through sign language and some pidgeon, which I understand. I am told the hotel is just about a mile and a half from the airport on the end of the island. I am told a bus of sorts will arrive soon from the hotel and to just relax. Not caring to walk, I stand outside and the natives and I watch each other. This is done frequently in these places. The bus soon arrives — it is a large van with the glass out of the windows and the driver is a smiling barefoot native. Taking my baggage — there are no red-caps — I gently carry and place it on the bus. Then as if everyone else is all at once urgently making their move, they just toss all the baggage and boxes aboard filling all the seats with suitcases, boxes and produce. With no seats left to sit on I throw myself on top of the whole sticky mess and off we go to the best, and only, hotel on the island of Nauru.

We pull up to the hotel about 2 p.m. and even though we were fed aboard the flight I am famished. I head for the dining room, but alas it is in the English tradition and meals are only served at specific times — three times a day — and I have missed the 12 o'clock meal. The next service is not until 7 p.m. What makes matters worse it is the only restaurant on the island, except for a couple of "joints" about two miles along the waterfront which serve oriental food — that is if they decide to stay open. The clerk speaks excellent English and I am told she is from Australia as are most of those in government on the islands as well as the pilots who fly for Nauru Airlines. I find the clerk quite helpful and she contacts the cook about my predicament. The fact is I am very hungry. I manage to talk the restaurant people into a salad which will tide me over until dinner. Then off to the bar for a cold drink.

The best source of information is a bartender and from him I learn much about this unusual place.

Nauru is an island about three square miles in area which has been made up of bird guano. The delightful subtance, after many years, becomes phosphate (fertilizer) and here is a whole island of it. The phosphate is sold and the entire population shares in the profits. Each man, woman and child receives about seven thousand dollars per year as their share. The money, however, is reinvested in many ways: hotels, airlines, buildings, etc. This investment is a hedge to when the phosphate runs out. Even with this income, there is a sense of timelessness about the place. Most of the people live in shacks with no windows; they need none. Many pigs run wild and palm trees are everywhere. There is a tennis court in back of the hotel but I wonder who may use it as it never was occupied during the five days I spent there.

The bartender brings me a cold beer and I meet an official from the government of Tarawa who is also having a cold one. He tells me that recently while excavating for a sewer on Betio atoll, needed because of a recent epidemic of cholera, an amphibious tractor was uncovered and hauled out of the grave where it lay buried for thirty six years. Upon bringing the tractor to the surface, they found it contained the remains of three

United States Marines. I vow I will look into this when I land on Tarawa.

Walking along the beautiful tropical beach, a native stops me and asks me to read the directions on a bottle of medicine he has been given by the doctor for an infection. Always glad to oblige, I do so. I learn he is from Guadalcanal and is one of the crew on the freighter in the harbor. When he learns I am going to Guadalcanal, he insists I give his name "Wally" to anyone I meet. He says everyone on Guadalcanal knows him and I will receive lots of help. Thanking him, we part; he for the freighter and I for the hotel.

The walk on the beach has tired me and I decide to lay down as I haven't had any sleep since Sunday night, the ninth of December. It is now Wednesday, the twelfth. In crossing the date line I have lost a day so actually it would only be the eleventh, but forty eight hours is still a long time.

Perhaps it is the anxiety or anticipation of what this long-promised journey holds in store that robs me of my sleep and rest. After all it has been over thirty six years. This may be a part of it or I subconsciously may be afraid to close my eyes and slip into dreams that have plagued me lately. Anxiety, anticipation, the dreams are so inexorably linked.

Being here is almost like being a part of an old movie. The tropical heat, the graceful palm trees waltzing in the wind to the music of the blue Pacific as it laps and beats the rocks along the shore, are the ideal setting. The hotel room itself, with the big four-bladed fan lazily going around, plop-plop-plop, is like an old Peter Lore thriller. Outside a tropical rain is almost putting you in a hypnotic trance as it beats down unmercifully. I can't shake the feeling that it is more like the heavens are perspiring. It is so hot! Rest does not come easily.

Dinner is served at the proper time; it is 7 p.m. The dining room is now open on this island that otherwise time forgot. The banker from Guadalcanal, Nicholas Maravoy, invites me to dine at his table and it is a real pleasure. The dining room, with linen tablecloths, linen napkins and crystal glassware, is magnificent. The service is by waitresses dressed in lava lavas. Somewhat like a sarong only they have no resemblance to Dorothy Lamour. They are short and bulkily built, speak little English and move very slowly. The food, however, is superb. I dine on veal cordon bleu with fresh sweet strawberries for dessert. Boy! Fresh strawberries in December! What a treat.

The cook is French and does an excellent job. As for the bill, when it arrives it is hard for me to believe I have dined so elegantly for only six dollars and no tipping allowed.

My stomach is now full. I stand looking out the window for a long time. The hotel is on the shore of the Pacific Ocean and the blue waters below the heavenly sunset, with the swaying palm trees in for foreground, create a scene so electrifying I have a hard time returning to normal. Still staring across the Pacific after the trance is broken, I silently pray my mind will also be full so I will be able to forget the horrors of the past.

CHAPTER II

NOSTALGIC MEMORIES

It is Thursday, December 13, 1979. Today I will land on Tarawa. That is if the Nauru Airlines stay on schedule. I will reach that small spit of coral which lays imbedded in my mind by tomorrow. Suddenly I am wide awake and it is only three a.m. Often during this past night I was suddenly awakened with fitful jerkings, unexplainable, but as if the spirits of my departed buddies are calling me, beckoning me to their hallowed ground, "Tarawa."

Outside the window of my room I can see the tall graceful palm trees gently swaying with the wind along the shore. The blue Pacific glistens in the moonlight as it dances and rolls to the tune of the four-bladed fan overhead, "plop-plopity-plop-plop-plop," with each revolution.

All of my thoughts are consumed by, Tarawa, "Tarawa Tomorrow." It is almost as if a dream I can see the waves crashing against the Higgens boat that held my buddies and me, we were waiting for one of the remaining amphibous tractors, "Alligators," to take us ashore, ashore into the gunfire of the enemy — the first wave.

I am bothered this night with the same feelings as that night thirty-six years ago, a night when no one slept, and anticipation ran high.

Suddenly, outside the night sky only moments earlier calm and black, now afire with a tropical storm banging and exploding as the fury of hades. It is nature gone mad and utterly wild as with the strength of "Hercules," spewing bolts of lightening stored for a lifetime and suddenly, upon release, flashing and crashing in unison. I ask myself, "Are my departed comrades welcoming me back to witness their last days on earth as mortals?" Answers are slow in coming, I would take an oath — looking down on me are Sgt. Slaughter, my platoon leader; Sgt. Brakeen, squad leader; Pfc. Plunkett and Pvt. Peterson, my close buddies, lost at Tarawa along with many others. Shivers run up and down my spine, not cold but warm shivers as though a signal approving my returning to this hallowed ground. Then almost as suddenly as the storm appeared, it vanished out to sea, leaving in its wake a calmness, and an eerie feeling, totally unexplainable.

I attempt to bring myself back to the present, but the images are slow to fade. My mind again wonders and wanders over what secret the beaches of Tarawa hold in store for me. "Will I be able to unlock that secret? How will they look?" It has been nearly four decades.

Will it have changed? These questions and many more occupy my thoughts over the next few days.

Finally sleep comes, it is an intermittent sleep, and it is six a.m. before I become fully conscious. Air Nauru won't leave for Tarawa Atoll until 12:45 p.m. but I have so much to do, yet I have nothing to do but wait.

I am to spend the morning at a lovely breakfast, getting ready and visiting with visitors I have met from Burma who have also spent the night. It is never a dull moment on those far off islands as everyone has an interesting story to tell.

The visitor from Burma is a lady of about 40 years old. She has several trunks and six children, all of whom she claims.

As the author boarded this converted landing craft which serves as the main link to Betio from the rest of the Tarawa Atoll he wondered if it were possible this was one of the crafts used in the invasion.

She is an Anglo native mixture and spends her time between Burma, Shanghi, China and Guadalcanal. She had some very interesting stories to tell bordering on intrigue, pioneering and family life.

Arriving early at the airport the time is wasted as they have one speed and it is "SLOW." Finally at about 1:45 we are allowed on board the Boeing 720 for the flight to Tarawa Atoll. These places that time has forgotten still have the modern methods of flight even though the plane only schedules one trip a week. As we are winging close to the Gilberts, I remember looking out the window of the plane at the dark Pacific, appearing and disappearing through the mist. I couldn't actually see familiar sights but the tableau was suddenly sharp and clear. I had been here before!

Approaching low over some of the atolls, our plane makes a perfect landing at the airport on Bonriki, the only commercial airport in the Gilbert Islands. As usual in these far off places, all the natives for miles around are happily smiling and welcoming everyone just by their presence. The turnout is remarkable and makes one feel a warm glow even if you don't know any of those smiling faces.

Finding my luggage is not too much trouble as mine is distinctive in that it is new and natives getting off are carrying mostly cardboard boxes and radios purchased on other islands. It is with difficulty that I am able to locate a motor car, which will take me to the atoll of Bikinabeau, a distance of about eight miles across the narrow road which has been built from atoll to atoll. There I have reservations to the one hotel on the chain of islands which are called the Tarawa Atoll.

The car is called a Mini Moca, from Australia. It is an open vehicle resembling an old Army Jeep, only one half as big, like a toy car. A shipment was sent to the U.S. for sale, but were ordered destroyed due to the safety or I should say, non-safety of their operation.

After checking in with a native who is not the best at English, and I not the best at understanding him, I go to my room where I find it really wouldn't have mattered to not have had reservations as there is always plenty of rooms. Only four were in use during my stay except when unexpected visitors came by, which I will write about later. My arrival here on Bikinabeau is Friday, December 14, 1979. Soon I will take a ferry to the Atoll

Part of the Atoll "Tarawa" leading to Bairiki from where the ferry departs for Betio.

A view of Betio, Tarawa from the ferry on the trip from the closest island, Bairiki, 1979.

of Betio, the island where so many of my friends died, so long ago.

It is a difficult time for me. After so many years, the reality of these moments attack swiftly.

Last night on the island of Nauru, I dreamed of dying. It was a pleasant experience, like a relief of tension or a load being lifted. As I faded away, in my dream, my last words were: "I love you, I love you." A wave of unconsciousness swept over me and I fell to the floor. Someone unknown, however I felt a great reverance for him, came into the dream and picked me up. I remember no more except it was a pleasant, relaxed experience. I am not afraid. I am at complete peace with myself.

After falling asleep again another dream entered my subconsciousness. We were again at war. A vivid dream; it strikes deep. A final release. I am awake to see Betio.

Breakfast in the dining room is a pleasant experience. The natives, I understand, are sent to Fiji for two years to learn the art of being a good waiter. It is a sought-after position and when they return their pay is forty cents an hour. Tipping is taboo, yet they stand so straight next to you, granting your every wish, proud of their job. A lot of waiters and waitresses in this country could take lessons from them.

Today on Betio I will be witness to much drama. But my first meal proved to be light-hearted. Eating in the native establishments was always to be a charming blend of western civilization and island culture. The waiter, a bare-chested native with a lava-lava cloth around his waist, took my order. He soon returned with my meal on fine dinnerware and placed it on the linen tablecloth. The food was well prepared with one exception, the toast. I am not particularly finicky. I'd been pleasantly surprised at the quality of services in these isolated areas.

But the toast. If there is a quirk in my eating habits, it is the need for warm toast at breakfast. It just didn't seem right to start this day, any day, with cold toast. With what I hoped was tact, I asked for more toast. Immediately the waiter ran to the kitchen. There the cook held the bread over the open flames of the gas store, one side at a time. While one side browned, the other cooled. I watched through the doors of the cooking area and resigned myself to having toast half-warm at best.

I had not figured on my waiter's ingenuity. As soon as both slices were browned on one side, the water snatched them from the flames and put one under each bare arm. Running to my

Betio, Tarawa Atoll, from the air, 1979. Total land area is one-half square mile. Note: The highest point of land on Betio is only about 6 feet above sea level.

table with a large, satisfied smile, he took them from their warming spot and placed them on my plate. Warm!

Who could complain about such a single-minded desire to please a patron? It was difficult not to chuckle. It was my first breakfast in years that did not include eating warm toast, but it was not on my plate when he returned. I owed him that much.

I leave to share a ride in another motor car for the trip to the ferry landing on Beiriki, an atoll about 11 miles from the hotel.

I arrived at the ferry landing amid a downpour. You would never believe how hard the rains come. I had been there before yet I was amazed to see rivers of rain. Then all at once the rain stops and within a couple of hours everything is as dry as before.

The ferry to Betio is a converted old Navy L.S.T. I wonder as I climb aboard, if it is one of those used in the invasion so many years ago. The only change made to covert it to a ferry, is a tarp stretched across the front, more to shield a vehicle that came aboard than to protect the walk-on passengers from the scorching sun.

In my mind I can visualize thousands of ways the islet of Betio may have changed, but I wonder, what will it really look like? How has the passing of so many years changed it? With my eyes closed, I see a bleak small island with the vegetation gone and the palm trees shattered and torn. The sound of Japanese rifle and Nambu machine gun fire rings in my ears as thousands of bodies lie bloating in the hot sun on the once white coral. The stench is unbearable. The pier, afire, thrusts into the at-last placid lagoon. An ominous calm surrounds it. About three-hundred yards out in the lagoon, a grounded freighter rusts, hiding on deck Japanese soldiers who swam out during the night and are firing anti-boat guns at the incoming Higgens boats and amtracs. The beach is factually lined with wreckage of these landing craft as well as grounded tanks and tank lighters.

I shake my head freeing myself of those horrible thoughts and then I am aware I am being watched. About thirty-five natives on this small ferry have been giving me the once-over. I take it as a friendly gesture, all smiles, and talking in their native language, Gilbertese, which I have a hard time understanding. The weather is hot and with the crowded ferry it seems hotter. Finally several of the natives revert to Pidgin English and I am aware what they are talking about. They have been told by someone that I am a former fighting man who came back to the island where many of my comrades were killed in the "Battle of Tarawa."

The ferry ride is only about three fourths of a mile as the crow flies but the ferry isn't a crow and swings a wide arc out into the lagoon to avoid the coral reefs. The trip takes a full forty-five minutes. With my eyes straining, I can see the beak of the island with a gun still in its mount. Then, in my mind, there is a huge explosion. It is November 20, 1943. I am in an amtrac racing for the beach. A heavy cruiser belched a salvo and at the place I had been looking, a large column of black smoke erupts and flames and debris boils up into the atmosphere of death . . . death . . . death. Yes, I see death in all directions.

Such a small place, Beito, like Gettysburg, a compact hell. If Betio could be described on November 20, 1943, it would be like a Nova, the flames and energy of a star dying. These are men dying; sons, brothers, fathers and buddies.

The battle for Betio on the Tarawa Atoll, an island of just about one-half square mile, had eight-thousand casualties. More than three thousand Marines were killed or wounded and nearly five-thousand Japanese died, in a seventy-six hour "War within a War."

Time magazine, shortly after the assault, commented: "Last week some 3000 United States Marines, most of them now dead or wounded, gave the nation a name to stand beside those of Concord Bridge, the Bon Homme Richard, the Alamo, Little Big Horn and Balleau Woods. It is called Tarawa."

A great hue and cry was heard in the congress of the United States. An investigation was called for, but as usual, while congressmen talked, a war continued to be fought and men continued dying. Much was learned from that assault against the best Japan had to offer and it was another lesson that formed the text which made the war come to an end much quicker.

As United States Marines, we are taught one important thing: to get it over with as soon as possible. Never wait for the enemy to regroup or reinforce himself. A lot has been written praising this type of action and much has been written condemning it, but it is the end of the war we all seek.

For you to better understand the people, the Gilbertese, I have added to my book some of their history, their creation and their beliefs and an insight as to why they believe as they do.

First let us look at their customs. Then I have devoted some space to tell of their early involvement in the war; a war not of their choosing.

This is a true story and not to be confused with a lesson in history. It is a story I have tried to tell on a personal basis and attempted to capture the highs and lows of the war in the Pacific and to express, in words, what it means for a young man to be thrust into the jaws of death before tasting the fruits of life.

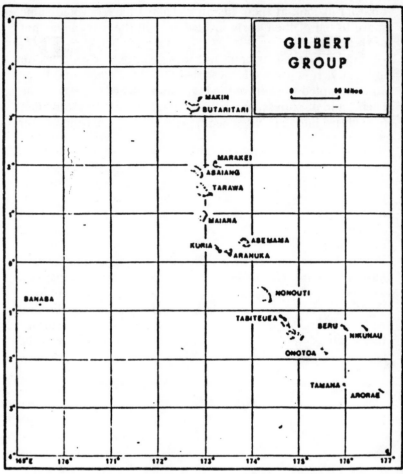

Formerly Gilbert Islands, now Kiribiti Nation.

CHAPTER III

"INNOCENTS ABROAD"

As a prelude to the telling of the horrible battle which tore the bowels from the tiny atolls of the huge Pacific Ocean it is necessary that you understand more fully of the death and destruction which took place in those far away places, and for you to know something of the life and customs of those innocent natives who live on those islands as well as the part they played in the drama fought inside their homes during the "Battle of Tarawa."

The Gilbert Islands consist of sixteen groups, or atolls and they roughly encompass over one million square miles of ocean. Within this group there are about 146 occupied islets which have a combined population of only fifty-four thousand natives. The most heavily occupied is South Tarawa which boasts of four-thousand two-hundred natives per square mile. These atolls have no fresh running water. Rain water is gathered in large storage tanks. They have no septic tanks. Outhouses are built over the lagoons. And they have no electricity. They only have one another.

The natives govern themselves by their own laws, customs and their particular culture. Some of these customs and cultures I will try to relate here.

In story telling the history of the Gilbertese people, native lore has been passed down from one generation to another. Some of the natives tell the stories better than others and some embellish in the telling, but basically, I found the stories to be quite similar whomever told them. The only difficulty I encountered was in the translation from "Pidgin English" which many of the older natives fell back to using while telling me "their story" and drinking Australian beer which, I may add, I was happy to provide.

The Gilbertese or Kiribiti (pronounced Karabass), are Micronesians of medium stature, straight hair, brown skin and dark eyes. One of the older natives, as he puffed on a cigarette made from the pendena leaf, a popular smoke among the natives, told me, "We call us Kaaenga, what you call family." When asked who wears the pants in the family, he said, "You mean who head man?" I said yes. He said, "Oldest man always head man; they have more brains. You respect that."

Just how they can survive on their small spit of coral sand was of special interest to me and when I told them of the United States and all the crops we grew, they all were wide-eyed. One young boy invited me to see his garden. Following him, we came to a pit dug about six feet down and at the bottom of the pit were green leafy plants. He said they were Taro plants and the trick to growing taro was to dig your pit below sea level and the sea water would turn to fresh water as it filtered through the coral and keep the ground moist making the taro root grow large and quickly. As the plant is harvested, a piece of the root is replanted and it takes the place of the root dug up giving an endless supply of taro from just a small garden. Taro is the equivalent of our potato and is one of the staples on the island. Fish, which is plentiful, is another staple.

Many other foods are gathered from the small island or grown in small plots of ground. Although they look very appetizing, I found them to taste unlike our vegetables. Maybe it is the chemical makeup of the land. There are no stones to clear off when they plant their gardens but they must be careful to shade the plants during part of the day and keep them watered.

I was warmly greeted by the family groups, or "Kaainga," especially by the small children. They were so adorable, so well-mannered and are in plentiful supply. What else is there for people to do in a place like this except raise children?

During the jawing sessions, I mentioned how I would love to adopt a couple of the little darlings. One of the oldest gave me a poke and half whispered in my ear, "Don't say that to any of the childrens mothers or fathers; it is the custom to give a child to one who is childless. It would be a terrible dishonor on the character of the family if they refused the request." He went on to tell me that often requests are made during early pregnancy, a long time before the baby is even born.

As we sat around the crude table consuming more beer, I asked many questions of the cultures and customs. From bits and pieces of conversation, I pieced together some of the following lore and customs.

After a couple married they were expected to have children as soon as possible. As soon as the woman became pregnant she was confined to her home as a safeguard against wandering spirits taking the baby from the mother's belly if she wandered too far away from her home. Many foods were forbidden the mother during this pregnancy, and any foods found partly eaten by rodents were strictly a "no, no" as it was sure to make the baby a trouble maker. They also believed if the mother ate any of the bait left over from fishing it would cause the baby to have twisted limbs.

When a baby was delievered a new clean mat to lay the infant on was provided by the grandmother. If the newborn was a boy the father, or an expert in the village, would cut the umbilical cord with a toddy knife, a sharp knife made from a sea shell. Many rituals, supposedly to have a magic spell, would be performed to insure the male baby would grow up brave and strong. If the newborn was a girl, a woman would cut the umbilical cord and give the rituals designed to assure the girl a better chance of being attractive and of growing up a good worker. After the cord fell off the baby boy, one of the grandfathers would wear the cord around his right wrist for three days and then wrap and store the cord in a safe place, for it was their belief if a rat would eat the cord the boy would grow up to be mischievous. In the event of it being a girl baby, one of the grandmothers would wear the cord around her wrist.

One of the most sacred ceremonies was the marriage vows. In many cases children were wedded even before their birth. The boy and girl would live in the same family from the time of negotiations until the marriage actually takes place. This is very soon after the time of the girl reaching puberty.

In visiting them, living with them and reading of them, I found the Gilbertese were extremely moral people. Friendly, warm, but with very high morals.

One of the older customs, but still remembered comes after the wedding ceremony and the vows are taken. Mats are spread around the floor of the house of the family where the newlyweds are to sleep. When the wedding feast is over, the boy and girl are called by the boys mother to go to bed and, of course, she remains close to the action to report on the newlywed's first meeting in the connubial bed. When the marriage is consummated, the boy calls for his mother who examines the mats for blood marks. If blood marks are found, she shouts to all members of the family, "The girl's a virgin." The uncles rush in and rub the blood on their cheeks and one of the uncles massages the new bride's muscles with oil to relax her. If,

Happy family on Betio, note the regrowth of the foliage since the devastation of 1943.

Native home on Tarawa, note trees still carry scars of the battle.

however, there is no blood, her parents are required to take her back; it is not a marriage.

As I mentioned, some stories are embellished with the telling and one elder had another story of weddings as passed down from many years ago. He told me, "After the feast is over, which follows the ceremony, the new bride and groom retire to the connubial bed." It was here the story teller told me this odd event took place. While the son is completing the marriage act his mother is hiding behind the screen, or grass partition, and calls out to her son, "Is she good, Son? Do you like it, Son?" and several other questions regarding the feelings he may have at the time. If her son, the newly-wed, answers with "Yes, she is good. I like it," the marriage is complete. But, if he says his bride does not please him sexually, the wedding is off. Sitting and drawing a big gulp of beer, I couldn't help but think, "Maybe these natives are not as backward as many people think."

The Gilbertese had many ceremonies . . . ceremonies for almost anything. The most solemn was the ceremony for death. Old age was a great honor and the feeling among the natives for many years was that death was the result of disobeying the gods. Many still believe this. Not many years ago after a member of the family had died, a mourning ceremony was held in which the body was anointed with coconut oil; oil which has been especially scented with sweet tropical flowers. The body was then brought into the Maneaba (the meeting house), and left in the center to begin decomposition. As the body rotted, the flesh was wiped from the bones and sometimes some of the relatives of the deceased would mix this liquid which dripped off the body with their food. It was their belief that by going this they would inherit the strength and wisdom of the departed.

After all the flesh had either rotted off or was removed, the bones were buried close to the family hut but the skull would be kept inside the hut. One of the strongest beliefs of the Gilbertese people is their belief that the spirits of the departed fly up into the sky and join their god Nakaa who is waiting for them while making nets.

As the natives told their stories it was as though I were a small boy again and I was sitting around a campfire listening to my brothers and uncles tell me of the beginnings and of our God in Heaven, Jesus Christ. These innocent, wonderful people, always smiling, always happy, had a beginning the same

"The Law." Policemen on Tarawa Atoll receive much training, but most of the crimes are due to drinking too much.

as I was taught of Jesus Christ; they were taught that their creator was the god Nareau. His full name was Nareau the Creator.

In the Gilbertese language the word Nareau means Spider. Although Nareau was a true god he could do many human things.

Nareau's origin is unknown. It is not even known from where he came or who his parents were. What is known of the "creation" and passed on from father to son is that he, Nareau, was floating all alone in space and sleeping. While sleeping he dreamed on three different occasions of someone calling his name. On the third call of his name, Nareau looked down from his lofty perch on high seeing a floating object suspended just below him. As our land is called the "planet earth," the Gilbertese called what Nareau saw "Te Bomatemaki," or the earth and the sky sealed together. When the god Nareau saw Te Bomatemaki floating below him he became curious. His thoughts included opening up Te Bomatemaki just to see what was hidden inside.

Using his tail, which was called "Kaweten Bukin Nareau,"

or, in our language, "the barb of the spider," Nareau walked about on the earth and sky which were sealed together. First he walked to the north chanting; then to the south, chanting; then to the east and then to the west, chanting with each stroll. Seeing no crack in Te Bomatemaki, he attempted to slit it open with his tail. He pried and pried until he had his tail inside and made a small hole. In this hole he placed his right hand and felt sand. He put in his left hand and felt water. Then, taking both hands, the one with the water and the one with the sand, he joined them together and made stone. Nareau then carefully layed the stone he had created back into the hole and said to the stone, "You, Stone, will stay there. I will call you 'Na Atibu' (the Gilbertese word for stone)." He, Nareau, then directed Na Atibu to lay and join with Nei Teakea (the Gilbertese word for emptiness), "And there you will bear a child which will be called Nareau Takikiteia (Gilbertese for Nareau the Wise)."

From this union of water and sand, Nei Teakea became pregnant and shortly gave birth to Nareau-the-Wise. All of this was done with instructions from Nareau-the-Creator.

At this time Nareau-the-Creator was on top of Te

"Maneaba," a meeting place for the native family as well as a play area for the children.

Bomatemaki, the earth and the sky, while Nareau-the-Wise was inside of it. Now Nareau-the-Creator commanded Nareau-the-Wise to stay on his father, Na Atibu, the stone.

Some time passed and Nareau-the-Wise lifted up the upper portion of the earth and sky. As he looked around he saw stiff bodies lying just beneath the cover he had raised. They were spirits. He needed these spirits to help raise the cover a little higher. He went to the stiff bodies and broke parts of them so they would be flexible and then could move. These spirits could not speak so Nareau chanted words working an enchantment to give them a voice. The spirits then began conversing with Nareau-the-Wise who at that time gave them names, some of which were:

Uka:	(blowing — the essence of moving air)
Karitoro:	(push into heat — the essence of energy)
Nabawe:	(antiquity — the essence of age)
Ngkoangkoa:	(long, long ago — the essence of time)
Kanaweawe:	(lofty — the essence of dimension)
Riiki:	(coming into existance — growing — the essence of pro-creation)
Auriaria:	(rising, coming from afar — the essence of light)
Nei:	(the octopus)
Nei Titubine:	(the sting ray, the cockroach)
Nei Towenei:	(the comet)

There were many other spirits given names by Nareau-the-Wise.

After Nareau-the-Wise had finished giving the spirits names he visited Nareau-the-Creator to seek advice on how to separate the earth and the sky. Nareau-the-Creator told Nareau-the-Wise to separate the earth and sky by himself first. Nareau-the-Wise gave an enchantment by uttering the following spell and managed to raise the sky a little.

The enchantment in the form of a prophecy went like this:

"Speak of the sky and move it.
Speak of the sky and lift it.
Rest it on it's pillar (the tree of life).
May fruits of this, my scepter, come forth.
Speak Riiki. Speak Tituabone
For Samoa, the first land,
And Beru the second land."

The version of which land was created first differ. It depends who tells the story. Some say Beru and some Samoa while others say Tarawa or Tabite Uea.

The enchantment worked a little for part of the upper portion of Te Bomatemaki, the earth and sky, lifted. By this time the crowd of spirits were able to speak a little and were given instructions to push upwards all at once which they did, shouting while lifting, the phrase: "Let's push together, oh!"

The spirits succeeded in raising the sky a little higher but Nareau-the-Wise wanted it even higher so he called on another spirit, Kanaweawe (lofty) to alone lift the sky. Kanaweawe succeeded in lifting the sky to his full height but that was all the higher he could go.

Nareau-the-Wise then called on the spirit Riiki who had the power to grow. Riiki was lying on his stomach and said he was hungry. With that Nareau-the-Wise went over to the spirit Nei Kiki (the octopus) who until that time had ten legs. Nareau-the-Wise tore off two legs from Nei Kiki and fed them to Riiki, leaving the octupus with eight which is carried over even today.

While Riiki was eating the octopus legs, Nareau-the-Wise was tapping words of encouragement on his chest. Then when Riiki finished eating, he lifted the upper portion of Te Bomatemaki (the earth and sky) while Nareau-the-Wise ran to the North assisting him by chanting words of encouragement. As the upper portion raised, he ran to the South where another verse of encouragement was chanted and the same with the East and the West. Thus the crowd of spirits could now move freely about and at the same time North, South, East and West were created. One important element was missing. It was so dark no one could see with much clarity.

Nareau-the-Wise went to Nareau-the-Creator appealing to him in his lofty perch above Te Bomatemaki to rid the place of darkness. Nareau-the-Creater then ordered Nareau-the-Wise to slay his father Na Atibu (the stone), saying from his body there would come sufficient light. Nareau-the-Wise obeyed and slew Na Atibu (his own father), and laid his body so his head faced east. Nareau-the-Wise pulled out his father's right eye and threw it in the eastern section of the sky. This became the sun. He then pulled out his left eye and threw it into the western section of the sky. This was to be the moon to help the sun give light. He then tore out the rib section of his father Na Atibu and threw it into the middle of the sky where it shattered and became the stars.

Now for the creation of the weather: With that Nareau-the-Wise tore his father's right hand off and, throwing it northward, said, "Go. Become the northwind. You shall be associated with strong winds, rain and bad weather." He then tore off his father's left hand and threw it southward saying, "Go and become the southerly wind and you shall be associated with fine days for navigation." Tearing off the right leg and throwing it westward, he said, "Go and become the west wind and be associated with rough and stormy weather." The left leg he threw into the easterly sky saying, "Go and become the easterly wind and be associated with fine days for navigation." Nareau-the-Wise then gathered up all of his father's intestines and threw them straight upwards. They later fell to earth becoming people. The spine and remnants of flesh and skin remained to become the tree of life and Samoa, the first of all lands.

Nareau-the-Wise then went to Riiki and asked him to raise the sky as high as possible. Riiki obeyed and tried to raise the sky with all his power. At that very moment Nareau-the-Wise stamped hard on Riiki's tail causing him to jerk with pain, carrying the upper part of the sky to it's present height and Riiki stayed up in the sky becoming what we call the Great Milky Way.

The earth, the sky, the sun, the moon and stars and the weather had now all been created by Nareau-the-Creator and Nareau-the-Wise and the entire world was inhabited by spirits. These spirits soon changed into half-spirits and half-humans. They procreated, settled in different parts and later changed into humans. This is the reason all natives on these islands have strong ties with the spirit world. This also explains when they die, their spirits rise to join their god Kakaa and help him weave nets. The Gilbertese people are of the belief that all races from all parts of the earth, black, white, red or yellow, had their beginning with Nareau-the-Creator.

"The Beach" after the battle.

CHAPTER IV

INNOCENTS AT WAR

We move now to World War II, the Gilbertese people and the part they played in that conflict. The war started in Europe in 1939 and did not end until 1945. On December 7, 1941 the United States of America entered the war against the Japanese after the Japanese sneak attack on installations on Pearl Harbor, Oahu, Hawaii.

During this time between 1941 and 1945 a lot of changes were made for the Gilbertese people. Japan began their conquest early, as part of the Gilbert Islands were to be in the southern resource area along with southeast Asia and the islands of Indonesia. These islands contained many raw materials so necessary for the economic welfare of the Japanese people. The Japanese military also needed to maintain their lines of communications and give protection to their perimeter, the reason for the South Pacific as top priority.

The Japanese dropped their first bombs in the Gilberts on the island of Banaba. It was December 8, 1941, the same day as the attack on Pearl Harbor. Banaba, being across the international date line, was one day ahead in time so it would coincide with Hawaiian time of December 7, 1941.

In the bombing of Banaba, the Japanese used a four-motor flying boat and dropped six bombs which fell on the Government Headquarters of Banaba. The bombs caused a lot of excitement but did little damage and no casualties. The island of Banaba lies between the Gilbert group and the Solomon chain of islands. At the time they were attacked, phosphate mining was going full bore. All the natives wanted to leave believing the Japanese would soon return with a landing party. A French cargo ship lay in the harbor and all of the European and Chinese population were evacuated, with the exception of two who stayed behind with the natives.

Within a couple of months the Japanese finally made the long-expected landing on Banaba and very quickly confiscated everything of value, rationing the food to the fourteen hundred Gilbertese and Banabaians who were left on the island when the others evacuated it. Many of the natives starved to death as rations were very skimpy. Some tried stealing just to survive, but if they were caught they were quickly executed by their Japanese captors. It was a really trying time for the natives. A lot of them went hungry. They didn't grow taro, their food staple, like on other islands. Just to survive many ate the roots of the paw paw tree and the Ren tree. Both plants provided some nourishment but were not very palatable. Within a short while the Japanese transferred all the workmen, with the exception of one hundred fifty, to other islands to work for them. The islands they were transferred to were Kusai, Nauru and Tarawa.

Near the end of the war, as the Japanese came to the realizaton they had been beaten by the United States, they committed many atrocities against the islanders. Many of the Gilbertese workers were blindfolded and with their hands tied behind their backs, lined up on the edge of a cliff at Tabiang, and shot. Two of the Gilbertese who had been blindfolded and were waiting to be shot, threw themselves over the cliff. They landed on the dead bodies of some natives who had already been executed by the Japanese. They stayed still until nightfall, then made their way to other islands and safety.

The natives have many stories to tell of daring escapes and long sea voyages. These trips were made in nothing but small canoes with no food on board and nothing but the typical "feather bait" with which to catch fish, their only food. The two managed to make the long voyage to friends on another island. One of the natives told of meagerly surviving for seven months at sea before being washed ashore at Ningo Island which is close to New Guinea. He later was flown back to Tarawa by the U.S. Air Force to recover.

On December 9, 1941, the fifty-first guard force of the Japanese army occupied the islands of Makin and Butaritari in the Tarawa group. Using about three hundred men, they took over the trading store and lived among the natives, dividing the natives into six separate working parties.

About one year after the Japanese took over the islands of Makin and Butaritari, August 7, 1942, as a diversion for the United States Marines landing on Guadalcanal, two hundred Marines of the 2nd Raider Battalion, under Colonel Evan Carlson, landed on Butaritari from two submarines in a daring raid. The Japanese soldiers had spent the night feasting and were using Gilbertese natives as guards. When the Raiders landed, they quickly captured the native guards, holding them overnight while they dug in. After the Raiders positions were set they released the guards with instructions to tell the Japanese of their arrival, which they did.

Heavy fighting erupted between the 2nd Raiders and the Japanese soldiers. The battle lasted three hours and was a victory for the Raiders. The tally at the end of the fight was 150 Japanese killed. In so doing, the Raiders lost thirty brave men. The next day Colonel Carlson removed his Raiders from the island with the exception of nine men. These nine men were no match for the Japanese numbers that later overran, captured, and beheaded them.

The Japanese planes, after the Carlson raid, made a bombing mission on the village of Keuna believing some of the United States troops were there. There were no Americans at Keuna but about forty natives were killed and over a dozen wounded in the bombing. When the Japanese left this time the natives believed they had gone for good so they took a chance and raided the stores; they were hungry. It proved a costly error for them as the Japanese returned the very next day, August 19, 1942, with a force of about two thousand men. The Japanese soon found out what the natives had done and the natives were all rounded up and lined along the road where it was believed they were to be shot for their indescretion.

That was the plan but a local trader came to their assistance. He was a Japanese shopkeeper who had lived on the island with the natives for a number of years and it was his plea for the lives of the natives that they were spared from a sure death. They had been given a reprieve but were quickly organized into working parties mending roads, building bunkers and wharves for the Japanese defenses.

Such a huge supply of sand was needed to build these defenses that the natives were ordered to dig a trench which was to be 35 meters long, 7 meters wide and 6 meters deep. The removed sand was used to build the defenses. This hole can be still seen today. As the digging progressed, word was leaked out that men from Butaritari and Makin were all to be killed; the trench was to be their grave. This mass annihilation was a planned extermination of all Gilbertese male population. In this way the Japanese soldiers would marry the native women, spreading the Japanese empire very quickly. The date of this holocaust was to be on Christmas day of 1943. This tale was

One of the 110,000 pound rifles imbedded along the beach of Betio. Note graffiti from the native children.

often repeated and was verified by a Japanese soldier who had befriended some of the natives.

The first visit to Tarawa by the Japanese military was December 9, 1941. They gathered everyone from the atoll to the wharf area and then proceeded to destroy all the transportation in the area. Some of the natives were killed in the takeover and all of the supplies were ransacked. The Japanese military came back shortly after the Carlson raid of August 1942 and stayed until they were destroyed by the United States Marines.

The Japanese fortified the island of Betio with everything they had. They were determined to protect it and keep it at all costs. They made emplacements and brought in, from the fall of Singapore to the Japanese, 110,000 pound, eight inch coastal defense rifles which were imbedded along the beach. Tank barricades and traps were built. Hundreds of coconut logs were cut and transported from other islands for shoring up fortifications. Large concrete bunkers were erected and individual rifle and machine gun pits were prepared. While these preparations were being carried out the United States Navy, by the light of a full moon, was bombing Betio at will. During these raids the Japanese hid their native workers on other islands.

Soon after the Navy sorties the Japanese made more landings invading most of the islands in the Gilbert and Christmas island groups. During these raids they captured twenty two coast-watchers from New Zealand, Australia and England. They were taken to Betio, Tarawa where they suffered many torturous hours before being beheaded by their captors.

A monument in the coast-watchers honor was erected by the natives in their graveyard and is one of the few graves which is kept neat.

Several coast-watchers were aboard our assault transports. They not only supplied valuable information but several made the hazardous landing aboard amphibious tractors. A record of one tells of surviving the landing making it over the sea wall for about 50 yards then facing destruction along with all aboard.

From information available, and information I was able to pry from visiting with some of the elderly natives, the Japanese on Betio numbered about two thousand laborers with another five hundred laborers on Butaritari. From the archives of the battle it is mentioned of only two hundred thirty laborers taken

Monument to nineteen brave British coast-watchers captured by the Japanese and beheaded one week before we landed on Nov. 20, 1943.

Japanese defense gun still intact on Red Beach Two after the passing of thirty-seven years.

prisoner by the United States Marines during the "Battle of Tarawa," November 20, 1943.

From a personal observation I saw only about thirty leave the island in a Higgens boat for a transport ship.

One other island, Abemama, was invaded by the Japanese on the 31st of August, 1943, but was cleaned out along with Betio during the battle of Tarawa on November 20, 1943.

These innocent Gilbertese natives had a great fear of the Japanese solider during the occupation of the islets in the Tarawa group. I can assure you after research this fear was not without reason. One instance of the brutality of the Japanese concerns the occupation of Banaba. Food on all the islands was of scarce supply for the natives. An example was made when three natives were caught stealing one chicken. The Japanese soldiers ordered the entire population of natives to watch as these chicken thieves were beheaded.

On Butaritari, some men were stripped naked and then tied to a tree and whipped with many lashes. Even on islands not yet occupied there was fear of the Japanese.

The natives I spoke with, for the most part, said the Japanese soldiers were polite toward women with the exception of where food was concerned. When the women cooked fish or taro the men of ordinary rank would just demand they be given it. The officers, however, they said, were much kinder and the higher rank the officer, the more kindness they showed.

Although the Japanese didn't occupy all of the islands, they visited most of them, raising the flag of the rising sun and giving the local governments orders. The natives insisted they only carried out these orders while the Japanese soliders were on the islands. The Japanese used some of the natives for coast-watchers, special guards and runners.

The general hospital at Betio was destroyed during the Japanese occupation and the lepers who used to be sent to Fiji were moved to south Tarawa in a colony. The natives said after Japan declared war on the United States, they no longer received many items they had enjoyed so much, such as tobacco. Ships that were often in the harbor trading with them no longer stopped. It was a very lonely period for them. Communications to other parts of the world did not exist anymore except in rare cases. Major Holland, head of the King George school, had a wireless hidden in his garden and continued to intermittently send out messages, but that was the only contact with the outside world during those days.

The first alert by those on Betio of any impending raid was when Admiral Powndale's fast carrier force sent planes, assisted by Army B-24s from Canton and Funafuti, and attacked Butaritari and Tarawa on September 18 and 19, 1943. It wasn't until November 20, 1943 that the United States Marines really struck the islands.

The original plan was for the allied attack on Japan to move through the Japanese held territories of southeast Asia and the coast of the Asian continent to Japan. Just after the Carlson raid, the Japanese changed their plan and decided on a drive through the central Pacific. The Japanese had, in the meantime, heavily fortified Betio in the Gilbert Islands as it was an important airfield, badly needed for their plans of conquest.

A final rehearsal by United States Naval and Marine Forces, in preparation of the invasion of these badly needed islands, was held in the New Hebredes island group. Hundreds of aerial sorties and heavy shelling by the Navy of the Gilbert Islands took place shortly before the invasion of November 20, 1943. Especially heavily hit was Tarawa and the atoll of Betio in the

Tarawa Atoll in particular.

Now, December of 1979 — thirty six years later — I am nearing the atoll of Betio again. The ferry taking me is in reality just an old tank lighter, i.e. used to bring tanks and heavy equipment ashore during war time. The voyage, about one mile, has taken the better part of an hour. On this ferry ride with me are many natives, smiling, laughing, really happy people. On shore waiting for the ferry to arrive are many more smiling, waving natives. There is not much to do on this island close to the equator except visit and fish.

The entire scene seems odd and slightly out of focus as we near the beach. The island of Betio is right in front of me. Not barren or foreboding but lush with foliage. As I leave the ferry and step onto the beach, there are no bullets, no sign of any enemy. Just friendly natives with warm handshakes and smiles to greet me. Even though the equatorial sun is unbearably hot, I hardly take notice.

It has been said that no man may step twice into the same river, for the waters keep moving. Could this be true? Many years have passed but now, in this place, many memories endure.

As I look at the beach and the remnants of that infamous pier with a lone Japanese gun emplacement still intact, marking the site, I remember that last boat ride to this shore on November 20, 1943. Many of my friends died that day. One who lived through it all comes vividly to mind. We called him "Chief." I will tell his story in the chapter "The Battle for Survival."

There were many moods on that ride. Some were quiet. Several were sprawled on the floor of the amtrac, reading comic books. Several leaning against the bulkhead quietly praying and few were whistling.

As we neared the beach machine gun slugs, hitting the sides of the amtrac, beat a counter rhythm to the "kaboom" of the mortar shells and the big "ker bang" of the anti-boat guns. As we threaded our way to the beach, using the old pier as our guide, we could hear, not only in front and sides but from the direct rear, field pieces firing from the grounded freighter in the lagoon. We were in a criss-cross fire with direct frontal fire from a Japanese machine gun.

The amtrac finally grounded on the corral sands of Red

Beach 2. We piled up and over the side. Many fell. More kept falling.

As I leaped over the side, a fragmentation grenade exploded to my left. Shrapnel had torn into my arm and hand. A Purple Heart, but it was no time to stop. Keep going or stay forever among the corral. It was three days before I realized how deep the shrapnel had dug into my hand.

CHAPTER V

A PRELUDE TO BATTLE

The place was New Zealand, the southern end of the North Island and the City of Wellington. We were the proud members of the Second United States Marine Division. The time was the 31st day of October, 1943 and we were listening to Tokyo Rose, a Japanese woman propagandist who broadcast to U.S. troops with what the Japanese thought were morale-shattering programs. She had just announced, and it was correct, that a complete new issue of combat equipment had just been issued to the men of the Second Marine Division. Toyko Rose had so much factual information about us; it was as if she had a direct line to Division Headquarters.

Our days, summer in New Zealand, were long. Yet our time was drawing short and on October 28, 1943, we began boarding the troop transports that were berthed in Wellington Harbor. The harbor was filled with ships waiting to move out together. Among the ships were a dozen APA's, one AP, three AKA's and many others necessary for the landings that were soon to take place. The 2nd Battalion, of which I was a proud member, boarded the troopship "Zeilin," code name "Blue Fox." Our new Battalion Commander, Colonel Herbert K. Amey, who was a look alike for Clark Gable even down to his well groomed black mustache, made a strong and lasting impression on me and I am sure most all of those aboard. To fill the rest of the space were joined with some of Regimental Headquarters Battalion, "Lots of Brass."

The troopship "Heywood" was picked as home for the Second Battalion Eighth Regiment, the "Middleton" carried the third Battalion Second Regiment and the "Biddle" was loaded with the rest of the Second Marines Regimental Headquarters Company. Aboard the troopship "General Lee" was the First Battalion Second Regiment.

All of these Marines aboard transports and ready to leave were referred to as Combat Division Two. Numbering was only a way of identification — we would all work together as one unit and numbering would only be academic.

In what at that time was referred to as "Transport Division 18" or "Combat Team 8" were the rest of the Eighth Marine Regiment. They were soon settled aboard the troopships "Monrovia," "General Sheridan," "LaSalle" and the "Doyen."

The "Third Transport Division," "Division 6," carried the "Sixth Marine Regiment" known as the "Pogey Bait Sixth," a name they earned when packing for battle and taking along shiploads of candy (pogey bait) with just a few bars of soap. At least that is the story that is repeated often. Not, of course, by any member of the Second Regiment!

Within two days the troops were loaded aboard transports, some seventeen thousand men and remarkably only 17 were AWOL, 13 prior to loading and just four after loading had begun. This was a record unsurpassed for troops going into battle, especially considering five hundred Marines had married New Zealand girls and many others were waiting for permission to get married.

Came the dawn of this, the 1st of November, 1943, we edged out into the the the stream of Wellington Harbor. Many Marines were lining the rails, blowing kisses to the loved ones they were leaving behind. I would imagine many a tear was shed behind closed doors as we sailed out of sight. Five hundred had married during their stay and in just a few short weeks, many of those young wives left behind would be widows.

Rumors spread that we were going to Hawks Bay for maneuvers but we knew better. We had been listening to Tokyo Rose and she told us we were going on a beachhead, and after all wasn't she always right? Soon we had passed up the lush landscape of New Zealand and were headed for tropical islands. Many thought "Wake Island" — the scuttlebutt was we were going to hit Wake Island. We moved through the warm waters, zig-zagging and when destroyers and other transports joined us we were even more puzzled. Maybe we were going to go directly to Tokyo!

On the night of November 6 we could smell the sweet odor of land and in the dawn hours we dropped anchor in Mele Bay, the island of Efate, south of Espiritu Santo in the New Hebredes group.

We of combat team two, climbed down the cargo nets draped over the side of the transports into the waiting Higgens Boats for practice landings on those hot sandy beaches. I had never seen so much wire strung out by a communications team at any time before — we spent much time in using hand signals to direct individuals, squads and platoons.

The island was a lot like Guadalcanal: coconut trees, cane fields and in the distance we could see a town. The town of course was off limits to Marine enlisted men. We found out later the name of the town was "Villa."

Around the corner of the island, closer in to the town, was a bay called "Havannah Harbor." As we got closer it was difficult for us to believe what our eyes were seeing. The bay was bristling with ships of the United States Navy. Now, we were certain this practice wasn't just to keep us sharp, something big was brewing.

Those ships really looked good to us, long and painted grey with huge guns sprouting from the decks. We managed to identify the old battleship "Maryland" and whistled with pride as we saw the firepower she was carrying. Those sixteen inch guns pointing at the horizon from freshly painted turrets looked all ready to fire like they were setting there loaded just waiting for someone to push the button. We were unaware at the time but it would not be very long before those barrels would glow red with the heat of hot shells heading for Betio.

Many practices were made in landing and communication during our short stay on those sandy coral beaches. Then on November 12, 1943, the word was passed to make ready to sail early the next morning. Scuttlebutt was running amok. Morale was high. We knew this was to be it but what or where or when? We had to wait for further word.

During that last evening several unauthorized liberties were made by the more daring. The natives would bring their dugout canoes alongside the troopship and for a couple of chocolate bars would take passengers ashore for a night of fun. One of the Marines who went and returned said the dimly lit bar was so dark he couldn't tell if his companion of the evening was man, woman or monkey. All he knew is he had a couple slugs of strong stuff, got a couple kisses and was left with memories to last a lifetime. For some of us that wouldn't be very long from now.

Early at 0600 (6 a.m.) November 13, 1943, as we left the harbor many of the Marines were lining the sides of the transports. Out came the Maryland, the old battleships Colorado and Tennessee, the heavy cruiser Portland, the light

Author

Portrait of a prelude to battle. G "George" Company, Second Battalion, Second Regiment, Second Division at Camp Pakakiriki, New Zealand. This picture was taken just prior to the boarding of the troopship "Blue Fox" for an assault on Tarawa. Note: in the background the tent and hills. The tents are what we lived in and the hills are what we lived on.

cruisers Mobile, Birmingham and Sante Fe and nine destroyers and two small ships whose duty would prove most invaluable in a short time the minesweepers Requisite and Pursuit. Up from Noumea, New Caledonia, came a weird looking ship, a sort of LST with shoulders. It's name, the Ashland (landing ship dock). Nestled inside were fourteen General Sherman tanks which soon were to be reduced very sharply in number. We knew we were to be joined by a large convoy but this number of ships, it didn't seem possible. Those of us who had spent some time at Guadalcanal didn't believe our Navy had that many ships left. It gave us a terrific lift.

Though we were crammed in, had not enough cots to go around, spent most of our time in lines and the sweat from below decks was a way of life, we rejoiced in the fact we were going to do something. Again the word spread all over the ship, it would be WAKE!!! It was our privilege to avenge Major Devereaux and those heroic defenders of Wake Island. If only it had been Wake. It may have been easier.

During the trip from Wellington I had carbuncles (ingrown boils) on my hip and instep of my right foot. They were miserable. The corpsman stuck a knife in the middle of each which popped with such fury the pus exploded all over the ward-room. I was just beginning to get around without crying with pain, but I wouldn't miss this trip for anything. Little did I know what was soon to happen. Many practice landings were held on Efete; principally we practiced communications, both with hand signals and radios. These were to become very valuable instruments later and could have been the deciding point of winning the battle of Tarawa.

Came November 14, 1943. D minus 6. Admiral Hill flash-ed this message to all transports: "Give all hands the general picture of the projected operation and further details to all who would have them in the execution of their duties. This is the first American assault of a strongly defended atoll, and with the northern attack and covering forces, the largest Pacific operation to date."

The large maps came out. It was not Wake. Many were disillusioned. Many were happy. The island we were schedul-ed to take was a long and skinny place looking like a lizard or a bird with a beak, upside down. The island's code name was "Helen." On it's northern shore were three planned lan-ding beaches, "Red Beach One," "Red Beach Two," and "Red

Beach Three." It had been no secret ever since leaving New Zealand; we knew we were heading for an assault on a beach. Now we knew the name of the beach. In the crowded and steaming cafeterias of the troop transports Heywood, Zeilin and Middleton, the commanders of we, the assault forces, were told the story of "Operation Galvanic." They, the commanders, told us everything that they themselves knew up to that time.

I smile smuggly recalling those last few days on New Zealand and of the girl I was keeping company with. Her name was Joan. A tall, lovely girl who lived with her mother. Joan took me on a visit to her aunt who was a "seer" and with the aid of tea leaves and cards could look into the future. I never believed in that mumbo-jumbo but as I recall the visit, she swirled the tea leaves and told me I could soon board ship and travel toward the United States, then in mid-ocean turn around and make an assault on a small island where I would be wounded but she assured me I would survive. She had been right so far. Let me hope her last words would ring true, "You will survive."

We, the men of the Second Division, Fleet Marine Force, had been chosen to open the offensive in the Central Pacific. Our target was to be Betio, or sometimes pronounced Bititu, an island in the Tarawa group of atolls, the code name being "Helen." While we were making our landing on Betio, the United States Army was supposed to be attacking Makin atoll one hundred miles to the south. With these island bases, we now would be within striking distance of the Marshall Islands, one more base needed on the way to Tokyo.

I shall always remember the briefing given us by our Battalion Commander, Colonel Herbert Amey. He wasn't one to do much talking, but when he talked we listened with respect. He told us like it was. No frills. His words still ring in my ears. "We don't know how many Japs are going to be on Tarawa. Our intelligence tells us there are a lot. Between 2,500 and 5,000. These men are extraordinary soldiers. Specially trained Naval landing forces. The equivalent of the United States Marines. They are the best the enemy has. The island is heavily fortified and although is is only 800 yards at its widest part and about two miles long, it is bristling with machine guns and some large coast artillery. Our immediate objective is to get the airfield in use at once."

We were told, with no stuttering, there were no plans in the works for any retreat. Our objective was the airfield in front of the assault. We have no word for retreat in the United States Marine language, therefore we will not include it in any plan. We were told this bluntly and, of course, we fully understood.

Further briefing by our commanders informed us that the Navy intended to put twenty-seven thousand tons, that would be five million, four hundred thousand pounds, of red hot metal on Betio even before one Marine went ashore. Up until this time, that was more metal than ever before had been concentrated on one target so small. Rear Admiral Kingman, Commander of the first support group, said of this amount of fire power concentrated on this small target only about one half a mile square in size, "We will not neutralize. We will not destroy. We will obliterate the defenses of Betio." If only Admiral Kingman could have looked into the future for a couple of days. Our Battalion Commander, Colonel Herbert Amey, said, "Don't expect all of the Japs to be dead just because they have been bombed and shelled. There is always some damn jackass that doesn't get the word and will still be shooting."

For such an important conquest, the assault plan was simple. At least on paper. A long pier jutted out into the lagoon from the northern center of the island and it would be the task of the Second Battalion, 8th Regiment to land just east of the pier, toward the smaller end of the island which would bottle up the Japs in that area. My outfit, the 2nd Battalion, Second Regiment, and the Third Battalion, Second Regiment would land west of the pier making an assault straight across the airfield to the opposite shore. Colonel Herbert Amey, our Battalion Commander, said of this plan, "We are very fortunate. This is the first time a landing has been made by American troops against a well-defended beach. The first time over a coral reef. The first time against any force to speak of and the first time the Japs have had the hell kicked out of them in a hurry."

Aboard the transports there were some understandably unhappy Marines; they were to be held in reserve. Those Marines in the Second Battalion, 2nd Regiment, Second Battalion, 8th Regiment and Third Battalion, 2nd Regiment were extremely excited about this landing helping to shorten the war, about picking up souvenirs and going home to their loved ones. Not necessarily in that order, however.

That old bug malaria was bothering some of the old battle-hardened veterans of Guadalcanal and as we now were back in tropical waters malaria returned to attack much easier. Many of the old veterans had high temperatures for 48 hours but not one of them wanted to miss the "excursion" to see Helen (Betio).

Shipboard life consisted of an abundance of card playing, always a line for chow and the heat below decks made sleep often impossible. We were allowed all the saltwater showers we wanted; the fresh water was rationed and could only be used during rationing hours. Boy, what a long line during that time! Many of us spent considerable time studying the relief map of Tarawa. It became more and more confusing to me how could a small place in the middle of nowhere have any effect on winning the war. We were told at briefing the island was about three miles in size. We learned later it had less than one-half square mile of surface and the highest point of land was just six feet above sea level. At the time none of us (I speak for myself only) had any fear of what was to come. Colonel Herbert Amey had a way of instilling true confidence and of making us all feel at ease with what had to be done.

Much time during these days was spent sharpening our knives and cleaning our rifles. We also spent more time in letter writing and the closer we got to our destination the more letters that were written.

During these days aboard ship on many occasions we were sent running for cover when the loudspeaker blared out "CLANG, CLANG, CLANG . . . MAN YOUR BATTLE STATIONS! MAN YOUR BATTLE STATIONS!" We never knew if it was going to be the real thing or not. We even had a general quarters over a whale sighting.

Being sent below decks while gunnery practice was on, or on an alert, is one of the most nerve wracking times I can remember of my days aboard ship. Those old tubs shook and shuddered each time a gun was fired and you never knew three or four decks below if the plates would buckle. It could have been the real thing and a torpedo might come sailing in, pouring thousands of gallons of water at pressures so great you would be crushed like an egg shell if you weren't killed outright. It would be impossible to escape from a compartment with its watertight doors closed and locked. It felt more uneasy below decks during those times than ashore facing the enemy. At least on shore if you were hit you were on land but on a ship if the ship was sunk, where were you?

Two days before D-day the Cruiser Indianapolis joined the rest of the fleet and on board was Admiral Spruance. Our convoy made a wide swing arcing to give us a heading direct for the Gilbert Islands.

Those long days on shipboard, prior to the landing, were often times spent passing along scuttlebutt and misinformation (scuttlebutt is usually but not always misinformation). As an example of scuttlebutt: "Army bombers had received no anti-aircraft fire from the target "Betio." Was Betio to be abandoned? Then another story: "The Japanese had built a line of cables underwater on the lagoon side to stop us." We found out upon landing they had built many underwater devices to stop us, but, thank God, most of them were on the Pacific Ocean side.

Many religious services were held top-side that last night before D-day. I may add hardly any Marine or Sailor failed to show up for at least one of the services.

General Julian Smith, our Second Division Commander aboard the Battleship "Maryland," sent an inspirational message to all men of the Second Marine Division, which read: "I know that you are well trained and fit for the task that is assigned to you. You will quickly overrun the Japanese forces. You will decisively defeat and destroy the treacherous enemies of our country. Your success will add new laurels to the glorious tradition of the corps. Good luck and God bless you all."

After General Smith delivered his message I felt almost at ease. I felt a definite pride in being a member of the United States Marines. This action would be a piece of cake. They wouldn't send troops who had it so tough on Guadalcanal to any place rough would they? After all it was only a small island waiting to be taken.

Back on Efete in the Hebredes, where we had made our mock landings, at a fire support briefing for commanding officers, one of the "battleship commanders" had boasted, "We are going to bombard at 6,000 yards. We've so much armour we are not afraid of anything the Japs can throw back at us." A "cruiser commander" then said, "We are going in at 4,000 yards. We figure our armour can take anything they got. General Julian Smith, *our* commander, then arose and said in soft response. "Gentlemen, remember one thing, when the Marines land and meet the enemy at bayonet point, the only armour a Marine has will be his khaki shirt.' It was no wonder we Marines held General Smith in such high regard.

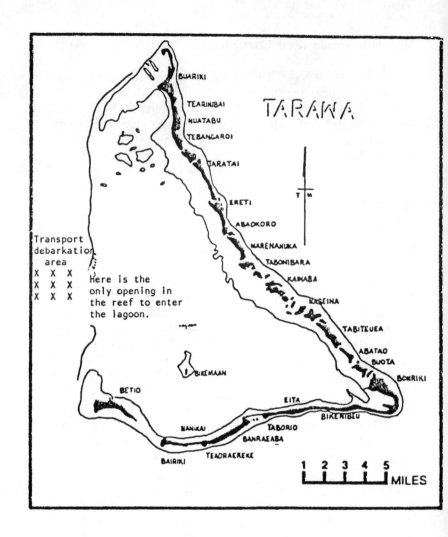

TARAWA

BUARIKI
TEARINIBAI
NUATABU
TEBANGAROI
TARATAI
ERETI
ABAOKORO
MARENANUKA
TABONIBARA
KAINABA
KASEINA
TABITEUEA
ABATAO
BUOTA
BONRIKI
Transport
debarkation
area
X X X
X X X
X X X
Here is the
only opening in
the reef to enter
the lagoon.
BIKEMAAN
BETIO
EITA
BIKENIBEU
NANIKAI
TABORIO
BANRAEABA
BAIRIKI
TEAORAEREKE

1 2 3 4 5
MILES

64

CHAPTER VI

"THE BATTLE FOR SURVIVAL"

November 20th, 1943 "D DAY". The time 0441 (or 4:41 a.m.). The Japanese had fired the first shot from the beach, then the U.S. Navy lights up the sky with a star cluster followed one half hour later by the belching of the 110,000 pound rifles taken from Singapore and imbedded in the coral along the rim of Betio's beaches.

We, aboard the transport "Zeilin," code name "Blue Fox," had just finished our breakfast consisting of Steak and Eggs, a far cry from "Guadalcanal," where it was beans, bread and gobs of coffee to wash it all down.

Our bed rolls had been deposited on deck where we were assured they would be brought in later. "That was to be the last time we would see them." With only our rifles and a day's supply of rations, along with grenades and ammunition, we scrambled down the cargo nets which had been thrown over the side and filled up the small boats or LCVP's (landing craft vehicle and personnel). These boats, were about twenty feet below the top deck of the transport milling around, when the waves raised and lowered them they sometimes came within a few feet of the deck. This is what made climbing down so dangerous. One minute the boat was directly beneath you and just as you let go of the net to drop into the boat the wave would drop fifteen or twenty feet, many legs were broken in this manner.

Our eyes were glued to the sky, awaiting the large group of B-24's that we had been told were to lambaste the island — they never arrived. Perhaps Hap Arnold was too busy to bother with such a small place.

Our first sight of any activity on that small atoll, "Beito," was a large pillar of black smoke curling up into the clear sky. The Navy planes had made a direct hit on an ammunition dump or exploded a gas or oil storage tank.

All of a sudden we were greeted with a granddaddy of a surprise . . . the Japanese were firing back. KERBLANG WHOP!!!

A huge water spout shot up not over 150 feet from our LSVP. My mind began imagining many things. My first thought was, "It is a short round from one of our own guns." Then another KERBLANG WHOP!!! The transports had already begun moving out of the line of fire. I then began to realize, "Colonel Amey was right. Someone on that island didn't get the word. They were still alive and their weapons were still in working order." Adrenelin surged through my body as the Higgens boat I was in made a mad dash for the safety of the transports. The front end squared off, banged into the waves and we were drenched. It looked like little ducklings chasing after their mother.

I believe I could have jumped out and swam faster, but this I declined to do. We all took to crouching lower in the boats, as if that made it any safer. If any of those rounds had hit us, the whole boatload of men would be gone in a flash. We had come into the lagoon through a small opening in the reef and now it looked like we were heading back out to the rendevous point beyond this reef. Lots of Marines became seasick on that ride and there were others aboard with just enough humor left in their confused minds to agitate those who became sick with stories of salt pork and greasy foods that helped make an al-

A view from the sun sights as seen by the Japanese defenders on Nov. 20, 1943. It's pointed out over the Blue Pacific, thank God. We made our landing via the lagoon opposite the ocean. Note the excellent condition after thirty-six years.

Picture taken Nov. 24, 1943, the day after battle. Note Burns Phillips Pier in foreground.

ready queasy stomach really upset.

Soon the transports stopped and began unloading again. It wasn't long before we were joined by some very weird looking boats. They weren't exactly boats; they were "Amphibious Tractors," able to run on land or sea. Transferring into one of those "amtracs" we were now ready for that "wild ride to the beach."

It was evident the beaches of Beito were not deserted. It was highly probable we wouldn't be back aboard ship in one day as many of us hoped for.

On the way in I remember looking over the high sides of the Amtrac, searching for any movement. On my immediate right was a beached transport. I was to find out later it was an abandoned Japanese freighter.

My mind was fully occupied with many thoughts and pictures of what we may find, hell!!! I had seen combat before and came through it, but what about John, the new replacement from the midwest. This was his first time out; he had joined us just prior to leaving New Zealand, only 17 years old, he said he had to lie to enlist. I thought, "How bad his family would

Betio, Tarawa Atoll, from the air, 1979. What looks like a building in the center is the new pier. Note: The highest point of land on Betio is only about 6 feet above sea level.

feel if they only knew how close their 'little boy' was to heaven or hell." My bunkie in New Zealand, "Brooklyn," we called him, was an old hand. He was only two years older than myself and he talked with such bravo. Now I detected his true feelings as I looked into his face and saw it twitch while trying bravely to smile but just not quite making it.

My thoughts were suddenly interrupted by the coxwain giving a load command, "Heads down, we're heading in. Make sure you have everything with you because you can't come back for it — get ready to jump when I give the word."

Coming in along the pier we could hear the THUMPA-THUMPA-THUMPA of the machine gun slugs hitting the armour plate, and every few seconds, the KERWUMPA-KERWUMPA-KERWUMPA of a mortor shell exploding alongside. "My God, My God," I repeated over and over, what the hell am I doing here." It was too late to change that now. Funny . . . I never thought of being killed, I don't think many do. YOU MUST BE IN A POSITIVE FRAME OF MIND. Think positive, never negative.

Looking around the Amtrac at the faces of the other seventeen men sharing that ride with me, there were many moods. Some were reading comic books, several were praying silently with eyes closed, a couple of fellows in the corner had a card game going. I was thinking, "how relaxed," but no one was really relaxed. It is like whistling while walking past a cemetery . . . a front.

As for myself, I became mute, not wanting to talk to anyone. My mind was going a mile a minute. Then about one hundred feet from the seawall the coxwain, with nerves like iron, gave the command to, "Make ready, we will be grounded in a few seconds." Then it was up to us to climb up and over the side.

Looking up from my crouched position I tried to look out the narrow slits in the front of the Amtrac. I saw the first carnage, the driver, that brave coastguardsman, had been shot in the head. A hole pierced the front of the Amtrac directly in front of his seat. I never had time to find out if the wound was fatal, but there was no panic. His place was quickly taken by another crew member who jumped in the drivers seat and, with the expertise of the well-trained man he was, swung the Amtrac sideways which allowed us to leave it without facing directly into the muzzle of the enemy's Nambu machine gun which was beating a deadly tattoo directly in front of us.

No one hesitated jumping or leaping over the side of the amtrac — it was the only way to exit as there were no doors. For a few long seconds you are a very visible target. A grenade exploded in the water beside me, imbedding bits of shrapnel in my hand which I scarcely took notice of until later. I hastily abandoned my pack with a days supply of food and I ran a few laps and then threw myself in a prone position in front of a coconut log emplacement forming a seawall. Looking back at the amtrac that had dropped us off I saw it was already backing around for another trip to bring in more men to feed the glut of war. Lying on the already stained white coral sands and half floating in the lagoon were four of the men I had just rode in with, slept with, prayed with and hoped with. I quickly counted the men from my squad who had made it to the beach alive — I counted only eleven. The horrible realization of what had happened struck me; the other five men in that amtrac on the ride ashore must have been killed or wounded as they tried to climb up and over the side and had fallen back onto the floor of the amphibious tractor.

It was an empty, yet euphoric feeling. I asked myself,

Looking down on the battlefield, Nov. 1943. The tail end of the islet.

Betio, the end of the atoll where the Japanese were driven in 1943 and committed suicide or were destroyed. Picture 1979.

The Lagoon Beach of Betio after the island was secured in 1943. Photo courtesy of U.S. Marine Corps.

"What's in store beyond the coconut logs?" I felt alive and invincible and yet as I raised my rifle to sight down the barrel I saw a trickle of blood which stained the stock of my "well-kept piece," and then I realized, "I had been wounded."

Quickly looking up and down the beach, it was not the tropical paradise pictured in the magazines — or as had been hoped for and talked about while still aboard ship. We had . . . to be sure landed on hell. God must have been millions of miles from here. Looking back toward the lagoon I could see no activity, no landing craft were coming in. My thoughts ran through an already busy mind, "Were we to be left here to be destroyed?" What was really happening in those large concrete bunkers? Thoughts flashed back to Guadalcanal and the feeling among the men when the United States Navy became invisible (late in 1942). The Japanese Warships had come close to shore and shelled us at their pleasure. We all thought we

The Lagoon Beach of Betio 37 years later.

had been deserted. On Guadalcanal, in the latter part of 1942, in the coconut orchards near the beach we could look up out of our fox-holes; the night would suddenly vanish as the flash of the muzzle of the Japanese long eight-inch rifle exploded into the blackness and a shell would come — woooshshsh woooshshsh or mptywoosh mpty woosh — as a round would go end-over-end. We had been told it was okay as long as you could hear the shells coming, it was the ones you didn't hear that got you. It was times like that when any statement of feelings is an understatement; these things can only be felt at the moment of their happening.

On Guadalcanal the Navy, thought destroyed, returned and were involved in a horrendous sea battle, visible from the beach. This battle saw the destruction of a large part of the Japanese fleet bringing in reinforcements. "Could this be a repeat?" My thoughts were caught short by an infiltrade of machine gun fire spitting directly in front of me out of a pillbox. We were immobilized, unable to move.

Many men had died that day and there were many more lives to be lost. One of the survivors comes vividly to mind as I write of this battle. We called him "Chief". His last name

"Over the seawall." Picture taken by Marine Corps photographer during fighting Nov. 1943. This is the same spot as below.

Author kneels in reverence on exact spot he leaped ashore from an amtrac on Nov. 20, 1943 at Red Beach Two.

Now dead, this once powerful diesel 671 from a landing craft was used in the invasion of Betio.

was Batchaddle, I never knew his first name. Most of us only knew one another by "Twitch," "Jonsie," or "Smitty." Batchaddle was a full-blooded Cherokee Indian from Oklahoma. He was strong, silent and well-liked. On New Zealand Batchaddle shared a tent with myself and six others. He was a good friend and a good Marine. We were the 3rd Platoon from 2/2/2 George Company — a proud, but scared lot.

Batchaddle quickly sized up the tough situation and hollered: "Stay down—I'll get those sons-of-bitches." Crawling on his belly (he was a large man), he carefully and methodically worked himself around to the side of the bunker from which the machine gun fire had kept us pinned down. Carefully and slowly reaching into his belt, he removed a gernade, pulled the pin, thus arming it, and with deadly accuracy, tossed it into a small slit leading inside the bunker. We all clawed deeper into the coral awaiting the loud exposion that was to come. There was none — just a small "POP", and instead of flying debris we watched as smoke billowed out from the enemy stronghold.

Chief had mistakenly grabbed a smoke gernade from his belt. The smoke gernade was a tool used for strafing which we would set off so the strafing planes could tell which way the wind was blowing and also to let them know where our lines were. That destructive, detonating, fragmentation gernade he had meant to use was still nestled harmlessly in his belt.

No one laughed or thought it a bit funny as we probably would have had it occured in a training exercise. We were engaged in a matter of life-and-death. Our enemy had been alerted of our intention and there was no time to delay; we miraculously reached the stronghold and swept over it. The large amount of billowing, black smoke had been just enough to disorient its occupants and we ended forever its deadly promise. The war, however, did not stop. It continued in all its fury. I would like to add, as a footnote, that from that day on Batchaddle was known throughout the Second Division as "Chief Big Smoke."

Crawling further inland from the beach (we were about twenty-five yards in from the lagoon), we could see in the lagoon Higgens boats beginning to arrive. It was hard for us to reason why, but the boats were unloading their passengers quite a ways out and you could see the men jumping over the side. Some of the men were not rising to the surface, others were wading,

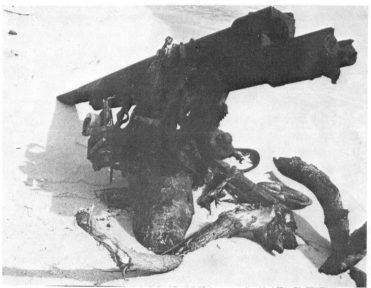

Japanese anti-boat gun from the "Battle of Tarawa" still on the beach of the Lagoon in 1979.

Japanese "Pillbox" on the end of Betio. This bombproof and bullet-proof "box" is made by sandwiching sand between two sheets of boilerplate.

falling, wading, falling. My mind was trying quickly to adjust to the sight I was seeing from a vantage point just a few feet above the beach. A huge explosion, from where a boat had been was just a rippling of water and debris, including broken bodies, floating toward the shore. These saviors coming to help us were being fired upon and some destroyed. It soon became evident the shells were coming from an old grounded freighter that lay in the lagoon directly to the rear of the arriving boats. The Japanese had anti-boat guns aboard the deserted ship and were using the situation to excellent advantage. They were mowing down wave after wave of United States Marines, but they still kept coming. The lagoon was now like a volcano, boiling, churning like an eruption.

Word was passed up and down the beach that our beloved commander, Colonel Herbert K. Amey, had been killed trying to get ashore through the Japanese barrage. My God . . . what a horrible feeling that settled right in the pit of my stomach as I asked myself, "What are we going to do without him?" "Who will take over and lead us?" We were certainly in need of someone to come in and take charge. As if an answer to our prayers for a strong man to fill Colonel Amey's shoes, Colonel Walter Jordan was chosen to take over. He had come ashore as an observer. Now our lives would be in his hands — and most capable hands they were — I was soon to find that out first hand.

Later we were to officially learn what we already unofficially new . . . that our Battalion, the 2nd, had landed on the toughest section of the beach. H. Hour was delayed from 0845 to 0900. It was actually 0910 when we finally hit the beach. The minesweepers, Ringold and Dashiel did a great job of clearing the path of underwater demolitions, but we were soon to learn that the Japanese were still in control.

Admiral Shibasaki, Commander of the Tarawa Defenses spoke with intelligence and honesty when he said, "One million men could not take the Fortress Tarawa." Admiral Shibaski never counted on the United States Marines.

It was of those first hours a correspondent was to later write: "The heroism of the Marines, officers and enlisted men alike, was beyond belief. Time after time they unflinchingly charged Japanese positions, ignoring the deadly fire and refusing to halt until wounded beyond human ability to carry on."

On Red Beach 3, the Marines had managed to wrestle their

*Twin Vickers that inflicted so much havoc among the assault waves
and tearing up the beach before the U.S.S. Reingold came in almost
scraping bottom to knock it out.*

Japanese revetment at Betio. Note twin barrels rusting on beach.

37MM gun across the reef after the boats carrying them had been sunk. There was no break in the seawall, so getting the guns over seemed to be impossible. That is, until several Japanese tanks appeared, then a cry went out, "Lift 'em over." With superhuman effort the two nine-hundred pound guns almost flew over the seawall. They were put into immediate service knocking one enemy tank out of action, the other fled.

The Japanese had built defenses unlike we had ever seen before, or could even imagine. Huge blockhouses, hundreds of pill-boxes, and row upon row of protected machine gun emplacements staggered to assist one another. There were fortresses made of sandbags, concrete and coconut logs. These fortresses could withstand rifle, mortar and machine gun fire and had to be captured by daring and dangerous use of explosive charges and flame throwers. Not one foot of the hot, dirty white coral we had landed on was safe or secure. It was necessary to resort to hand-to-hand combat to drive these sons-of-the-rising-son from their emplacements as not more than a rifle length separated us at times. If you were foolish enough to put your hand above the seawall during those first few hours, you would draw back a stub.

Looking out over the lagoon and the carnage displayed openly, there was still much more to come. You could see many Marines floating, bobbing with the surf. It was suicide at this time to attempt recovery of the bodies. You could see — and it was heartbreaking — the men debarking from the Higgens boats as they waded ashore trying to dodge the ripples which would seem to ebb and flow as the Japanese machine-gunner would raise and lower his barrel, then traversing in an arc one or two would be hit and disappear. Then a deep hole would claim another and he and his heavy equipment would be lost to the war; but, to his loving family back home only one thing would be told them, "Their son had made the supreme sacrifice."

The broken and dead palm trees were alive with Japanese snipers tied in them. Their rifles were taking a deadly toll on Marines lying in holes or moving forward. On the beach a pair of Japanese machine-gunners waited patiently until the Marines made it to the beach from the Lagoon and then open fired in a semi-circle of death, leaving their victims laid out on the coral in a fan shape to quickly rot and turn black in the hot sun.

If you can call being there lucky, most of the three assault

"By His Leadership — Many Marines Lived to Fight Again." Colonel David M. Shoup was awarded The Congressional Medal of Honor." —Photo courtesy of U.S. Marine Corps.

waves did make it to shore that first dismal morning even through the withering fire from Japanese machine guns and mortars. Our job was to try and make their landing as safe as possible so together we could take the island.

We may have been disorganized but, as Marines, we were capable of thinking for ourselves and still work as a team. The Japanese, thank heaven, were even more disorganized than we and they appeared to lose the initiative when losing their leaders.

Communications played a large part in capturing the one-half square mile of hell. Many of the radios were water-logged and therefore useless. One of the messages that did get through the first hour was the tersely worded, "Have landed. Unusually heavy opposition. Casualties seventy percent. Can't hold." Those few words were enough for some of those on board the transports, supposedly in reserve, to come to the aid of their fellow Marines. Some were committed and chomping at the bit, they started for the beach. Along with new fresh Marines, came the General Sherman tanks. Even though we had been ashore for less than an hour, only about two-thousand men had made it alive out of the estimated 2500 to 3000 Marines who stormed ashore into the withering gunfire of the enemy. No count was taken, but it would be a fair estimate to say nearly half of these two-thousand surviving Marines suffered wounds, but still kept fighting to complete their task.

In spite of all the caution, confusion, chance and casualties, the Marines were not fighting for their lives; they were fighting for the Second Marine Division and the whole Marine Corps.

Robert A. McPherson, the pilot of a small Kingfisher observation plane which flew overhead during the fighting, reported to Admiral Hill and General Smith and wrote in his log: "The water seemed never to clear of tiny men, their rifles held over their heads, slowly wading beachward. I wanted to cry."

We were in bad need of help. The lines of the wounded stretched along the beach for nearly fifty yards. That didn't include minor wounds. If you were still able to fire a rifle and hold it, you were on the line. Ammunition, plasma and much more communication equipment was in short supply. Word was passed, "Reinforcements were on the way." Two companies from the First Battalion, Second Regiment were coming in. Most of the amtracs were out of action so the reinforcements came in the Higgens boats. There was a lull in the action as these boats made their run for the beach and the ramp lowered, then WHANG!!!

KERBANG!!! From our positions, it sounded like a steel girder hitting concrete. Then one of the boats just disappeared; it had been there unloading one minute, then gone. All that remained was a large cloud of black smoke and, for a few seconds, a water spout.

Within minutes another boat vanished. God, how could you let this happen? They were needed. They were being annihilated even before they could fire a shot and, worst of all, there was nothing, absolutely nothing, we could do about it. The Japanese had one of the Twin Vickers, dual 4.7 guns, back in working order. It was on the end of the island. We felt helpless. Many who had faced the enemy all morning wept openly and slammed their fists into the hot sand. It did no good. Further disaster awaited other boats. One of the coxwains, when some distance from the reef, screamed, "This is as far as I go." He let the ramp down and a boatload of Marines, heavily laden with gear, tumbled into fifteen feet of water, drowning many. Other boats, coming in were raked with machine gun fire. One piece of luck: the mine sweeper Reingold with Cmdr. Ross Eastham moved close in and let off about twelve shots. But it had done a tremendous amount of damage before being silenced.

During that afternoon of the first day, nothing much happened on the beach, except maybe one-thousand or more Marines performed acts of bravery that would, in any other battle, have earned them the Navy Cross.

On Red Beach Two, Colonel Shoup was trying to make sense out of the battle while fighting it at the same time. The corpsmen and the members of the Marine band spent most of the day climbing between the seawall and racing around pillboxes trying to drag the wounded to safety.

The first evening, the sunset was magnificent. Maybe I thought it was beautiful because it could be the last one I would ever see. Most of us were lost that first night. I should say lost from one another. We sure as shooting knew where we were, we were at that place our mothers told us we would go if we didn't behave . . . hell.

We forged our way ahead for another 150-yards, then through the lone radio one of the men carried, came word. The Navy was going to strafe immediately in front of our lines and they wanted to know where our lines were. We were to put down markers to let the plane pilots know. Most of us had lost everything except our rifles and ammunition when we hit the beach. We did our best but apparently it wasn't enough.

Then they came, the unmistakable drone of planes overhead. All we could do was lay flat and bury our faces deeper and deeper into the hot coral sand and pray. Then came the "THUMP," "THUMP," "THUMP," of the fifty caliber shells slamming into the sand. I had seen death and destruction, bodies blown apart and, from a silent sniper's bullet penetrating the air, many good men cut down in the jungles, men who I shared my life with here in this lonely part of the world. The sight I witnessed as I raised my head was the most morale shattering experience I have ever witnessed or will in my lifetime witness. To my right flank three of the ten men in my squad were still lying flat with their brains and blood splattered on the hot coral. On the left flank, my squad leader had been hit in the chest. He was at peace with the world.

I stood straight up, disregarding the danger of rifle and machine gun slugs singing past, waving my arms, damning and swearing at those who dared shoot their own. I felt a wave of despair but it lasted only a few minutes; too much was happening. An island needed to be taken and I suddenly realized what an excellent target I was.

Shaking myself back to reality — no, it was not a dream, it was real — I knew by now that the Japanese aren't going to drive us off the island. Why? Because I am good and mad, damn mad.

Painfully, slowly, I manage to crawl, run and slide another fifty yards inland where I sight a building. It is wide open and looks deserted. We push on past this building which is the largest I have seen so far on this desolate atoll and just manage to dive headfirst into a bombshell crater as a line of machine gun slugs hit the sand in a deadly pattern. We are pinned down. I say "we" but I am alone. We have all jumped in different holes and, using our bare hands, scoop even deeper for we know the tall palm trees hold an execution squad, always at the ready for just one more trophy. These are Japanese soldiers tied to the tops of the trees where they await and pick and choose their targets at will, and it is hot. I am thankful for one thing at least: darkness is quickly approaching.

On this dark and foreboding first night, I was alone. Yet I was not alone. I heard a rumbling sound along with unmistakable sound of tank treads squeaking as they rolled along the coral. A feeling of relief flooded my body as I recognized it as one of ours. The name "China Gal" was painted on it's side. What a beautiful and welcome sight! The tank made a few circles with its turret and stopped just to my right where it became bogged down in the coral for a time. I was to spend a sleepless night as tracers, both Japanese and Marine, criss-cross in many patterns. Noises echoed through the night which were impossible to recognize or trace but still enough to turn one's blood to ice. That is if you were lucky enough to still have any blood left.

Dawn came early on the equator and during the night a half-track had made it ashore loaded with badly needed ammunition. I made a dash for the safety of the steel sides of the amtrac and found myself in a work party assigned to quickly unload the ammunition while dodging bullets flying in all directions. During the unloading several of the men beside me ran out of luck and they already had turned black and were beginning to bloat in the hot sun. I loaded a box of hand grenades on my shoulder. Just as I turned a machine gun let go with a blast. Slugs tore into the box. I threw it down and made a dive under the protection of the amtrac. I was lucky, several others were not.

Our mission was to secure the airstrip. It was directly in front of us. Tossing a bandoleer of ammunition over each shoulder and stuffing our pockets with fragmentation grenades, we slowly worked our way forward to about halfway across the island, just on the edge of the airstrip. We were forced to dig in as a fuselade of rifle and machine gun fire pinned us down. We made a dive for the only cover available, an abandoned shell-hole or a bomb crater. It is there I meet a giant of a man, a man whom I shall always remember, Colonel Jordon. Colonel Jordon came ashore as an observer, but quickly took command when Colonel Amey, our Battalion commander, was killed coming ashore that first day.

It is in my shellhole the meeting between Colonel Jordon and I took place. Both him and his runner jumped in on me unannounced. His runner had a PBX strapped to his back. He quickly took the initiative and issued orders for a squad to follow him across the airstrip. After exchanging signals to our objective, without hesitation, Colonel Jordon jumped out of the hole and, in a commanding voice, yelled, "Follow me." If there ever was a time we needed a man to admire, respect and follow without question, that man was Colonel Jordon. He led the way with his runner beside him and me along with the rest of the squad in hot pursuit. During that dash for the other side of the air-strip, I saw blood running down Colonel Jordon's runner's face, but it wasn't until we had crossed the strip and jumped into the cover of another shell hole that I could see where he had been hit. The projectile entered in the front, to the right of his windpipe, and exited out the back of his head leaving a gapping hole at neck level. It was at that moment the runner placed his hand to the wound. His hand was engulfed. The shock must have been too much for, at that moment, the brave runner drop-ped dead.

There was no time to cry, even if you wanted to. No time to quit or even re-group. We had been committed and must keep on going. We made it to the opposite side of the island where the battle came more into focus for me as I found many of my company lying dead on the coral sand. It had been just a little more than twenty-four hours since we set foot on this strip of land, yet the bodies had already turned black in the torrid heat. I was to wonder then, as I pondered later, how an island with less than one-half square mile of area could create so much havoc and destroy so many men. Was anything worth this sacrifice?

I never had much time for thoughts. We were to experience heavy gunfire from Japanese machine guns and snipers. Many of my buddies lay dead, many more wounded to such an ex-tent they lay helpless on the hot sand. I was lucky. I was to spend another night in a shellhole by myself.

Never before have I talked of killing or shooting anyone, although in a war it is a fact of survival. To survive in a war it must have happened. Many times during the war in the Pacific I came close to becoming a casualty, but the nearest I came to being skewered on the end of a Japanese bayonet happened that second day as fighting was from foxhole to shellhole and from behind coconut logs and bunkers. After a particular in-filade of machine gun and rifle fire, I had a shellhole picked out just off the edge of the airstrip. It was up, keep your butt down, run in a staggering pattern and make your dive for the safety of a hole. As I started my dive into what I thought to be the safety of a large crater, a Japanese soldier chose this moment to come out of the same hole I was heading for. We met — face to face! I had seen many Japanese soldiers before,

Picture taken in 1943 soon after the battle. Note gun back from the beach.

The same shore battery as in previous picture, 37 years later. Note how the island has shifted, the gun now is nearly claimed by the ocean.

but this one looked like a giant. He was at least six foot tall and looked like a small mountain coming toward me. We had been told on board ship that these soldiers were the equivalent of our United States Marines, but until then, I wouldn't have believed it. He had a fixed bayonet. I had lost my bayonet the day before. Both of us were, in all probability, equally surprised. I believe it was only because I was able to react quicker that I am still alive. I often have wondered what the odds would have been had I jumped in about two seconds earlier or two seconds later. War is indeed hell — but fate is the hunter.

During the battle many of the previously made plans were quickly changed to fit the situations as they arose. I was to learn later that the plans for the dispersal of tanks called for four tanks to be landed on Red Beach Two in support of my Battalion, the mighty Second. Four tanks were to be landed on Red Beach Three in support of Second Battalion, Eighth Regiment and six tanks were to be landed on Red Beach One, in support of the Third Battalion, Second Division. Shortly before 1000 hours, or 10 a.m., the six tank lighters lowered their ramps and dumped the Sherman tanks on the reef, just off Red Beach One, about eight-hundred yards from shore. The tanks began rumbling ashore under their own power through water that came almost up to the slits in their turrets. Tank men walked in front of the tanks to mark potholes with flags, disregarding the Japanese fire which was relentless. Four of the tanks dropped into holes in the reef and were stalled, but two tanks made it ashore. One of them was to be my comrade for the night, "China Gal." The remaining two tanks that made it to shore were knocked out of action. Major Ryan established China Gal on his flank which had been exposed. I should know; I was lying in a hole almost next to the old girl, "China Gal."

On the other beaches the landed tanks did well in knocking out the Japanese fortifications as long as they lasted, but it was difficult to operate a tank in blind fashion. Their vision is limited from inside the tank and soon both were put out of action by the 4.7 Vickers dual purpose guns, plus another tank was destroyed due to an explosion. By nightfall the only survivor of tanks on Red Beach Three was "Colorado," a Sherman tank. It was smokey, but still able to perform. This made China Gal and Colorado the only operating tanks out of fourteen that were landed, that I was aware of.

Several half-tracks made it ashore, but most of them prov-

"He gallantly gave his life." Marine First Lieutenant William Deane Hawkins, awarded the Congressional Medal of Honor Posthumously. —Photo courtesy of U.S. Marine Corps.

ed ineffective and became bogged down in the coral. They were mainly used for bringing in ammunition over the reef.

A word must be written here for one of the smallest, yet one of the most important bands of specialists on Beito, "The Scout and Sniper Platoon" under Lt. William D. Hawkins. They made a landing on the tip of the pier fifteen minutes ahead of the assault wave. The Japanese had a seaplane ramp near the end of the pier. Hawkins, along with four enlisted men and Lt. Leslie of the Engineers, fought their way up the ramp with grenades and flame throwers. They burned two houses, cleaned out a Japanese machine gun nest and worked their way along the pier until Hawkins felt the pier offered no more resistance. Hawkins then went ashore and was a major factor in blasting Japanese gun emplacements. The next day "Hawk" died, and in dying, won the highest award for bravery our government can give, the Congressional Medal of Honor. Hawkins was from Texas. As a youth he had suffered horrible, disfiguring burns over his body and was told by his doctor he would never be able to walk again. His mother didn't believe the doctors and she spent agonizing hours every day working his muscles and massaging him, besides giving him the encouragement only a mother can give her son. "Hawk," with the tremendous help of his mother and his devotion to a regimen of exercises, overcame this handicap, and to prove this to his mother and himself he entered all manner of sports in school and excelled in all that he did. When he tried to enlist in the service he was turned down several times due to his disfiguring scars. He persisted and was granted enlistment in the United States Marines where he again proved himself and excelled beyond the call of duty. What a great story of courage!

A lot of other brave men perished before Hawk, but when word was flashed from foxhole to foxhole around the atoll that "Hawk got it," the men seemed to fight with a renewed vigor. Some of us knew him. All of us knew of him. We all respected and admired him and we all knew he would be greatly missed.

Those men from Texas! They could run faster, shoot straighter, dive deeper and come up dryer than anyone else in the world, according to their tales. I well remember my platoon in boot camp. It was made up of mostly Texans and the better part of them came from Big Springs and, according to those who claimed Big Springs as their hometown, it was larger than Houston, Amarillo and El Paso all put together. It wasn't

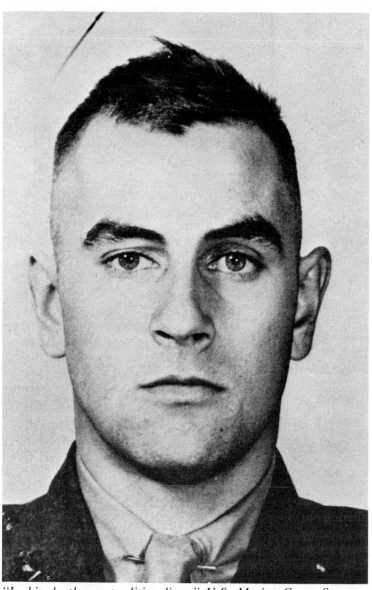

"In his death our tradition lives." U.S. Marine Corps Sergeant William J. Bordelon was awarded the Congressional Medal of Honor Posthumously. —*Photo courtesy of U.S. Marine Corps.*

until twenty years after the war when I went through Texas that I discovered Big Springs was just a small town. Even smaller than my hometown. Looking back, I would imagine every able-bodied man volunteered for the United States Marine Corps at the same time. I would call that a real tribute to Big Springs.

I must give acknowledgement to the bravery of the men of the Engineer Battalion. All of us who landed on Betio can attest to the effort it takes to jump over the side of an amtrac or, when the ramp drops in the front of a Higgens boat, to run out, and we were only carrying about sixty pounds of gear. The Engineers, in addition to the sixty pounds of gear, carried flame throwers with twin tanks loaded with Napalm, packs of high explosives along with many other devices to set them off. As these men hit the beach, their eyes would immediately size up the situation. They had had good training, they worked in pairs, one covering while the other threw in the explosive, more good training. After the charge exploded in the pillbox and a cloud of dust came rushing out, usually one or a couple of Japanese would exit running for what they thought may be a safer place than where they were. The flame thrower would be ignited and the Japanese soldier would explode like a piece of celluloid film.

When the fuel, napalm, ran out in the tanks you would see men run after these exiting Japs to get a better shot as they mostly carried Carbines and were not accurate unless you were close. Now that was not training; that was what I called courage.

There were many stories of courageous men during those three days of fighting. One story is of an enterprising Higgens boat coxwain from aboard the transport Zeilin by the last name of Stokes.

After making several trips via his Higgens boat with Marines, Stokes returned to the Zeilin with his Higgens boat riddled with machine gun fire. He patiently had to fight his way up the chain of command. Finally he reached Commodore J.B. McGovern where he proposed a bold plan to clear out the pier of snipers that were cutting the men to ribbons as they made their landing on Red Beach. He asked to be given a new boat and to be assigned a man with a flame thrower. He would take the boat down the channel, next to the pier, and the flame thrower would eliminate any Japanese that were hiding there. A Marine Flame Thrower team had already volunteered and was standing by. Commodore McGovern granted Stokes' request and the mis-

Maw of a concrete bunker. When the author brushed the ceiling many lead slugs, green with age, dropped to the ground.

sion was accomplished with the desired results and only minor casualties to the crew.

On the D Day landing we had two twenty-man sections of men assigned to the flame throwers. One of the sections, twenty men, was totally wiped out on landing. The other section had enough survivors to account for many positions destroyed by nightfall. These men were attached to the First Battalion, Eighteenth Regiment. When the word Flame Throwers is mentioned many people in armchairs and students who have yet to taste the sweetness of life, or the bitterness of death, refer to them as horrible examples of insanity. But those of us whose lives were narrowly teetering on the brink witnessing the long tongues of flame licking at the coconut log placements and seeing the Japanese running to escape, caught in a flame so hot they literally exploded thought, what a beautiful sight to behold. My only wish at that time was that we could have had hundreds more of those lovely, beautiful, flame throwers along with us on this island of death.

Another brave man to win the Medal of Honor that day was Staff Sergeant William J. Bordelon from Texas. Sergeant Bordelon was a member of the assault platoon from the First

Battalion, Eighth Regiment. The Japanese blew his amtrac right out of the water. He was one of only four who survived. Once ashore, Sgt. Bordelon instantly went into action. Using the two demolition charges he had made up, he destroyed two enemy pillboxes. As he was attacking the third pillbox he was hit by Japanese machine gun fire. Not stopping, he picked up a rifle and, covering a group of Marines who were going over the seawall, though seriously wounded, he waved off a corpsman who tried to administer first aid then splashing off in the lagoon, he went to the aid of another demolition man who was calling for assistance. He succeeded in rescuing two more from the lagoon but was not satisfied. Bleeding from his own wounds, but oblivious to the same, he prepared another demolition charge and, without cover, made an attempt to destroy another Japanese fortification. William Bordelon was caught in a volley of bullets and was killed instantly. There certainly are a lot of brave men from Texas.

Throughout D Day, November 20, 1943, the Navy destroyers opened fire on Japanese installations using a spotter on the beach for directions. Most of the shells were hitting right on

Another of the shore batteries manned by the Japanese lies rusting along the beach.

target and, with each volley fired, the destroyers would move even closer in to the beach. So close that many of us thought they may get hung up on coral or debris which covered the bottom of the ocean so close to shore. That first day finally ended, a day of carnage, a day when each square foot of sand was bought and paid for with gallons of blood and pounds of guts.

November 21, 1943 — A miracle, yes a true miracle for many of us on that atoll called "Betio." The morning of that second day was almost like a resurrection. We remembered that during the night each man — I know I did — made his peace with his god, and was only thinking of quickly getting the job done. I had carried a well-thumbed Testament since Guadalcanal, and it was very close to me. Every night as darkness fell, keeping my eyes wide open, I would say prayers for those who had fallen and for those still alive. Several times during the night I would repeat my "prayers," on the chance they weren't heard the first time. There was a lot of noise going on down here.

As the Japanese made their attacks and counter-attacks against our frail positions many of the men were about to sell their lives dearly, fully understanding that all sales would be final. Many Marines who were alive that day would never live to witness another sunrise nor sunset.

Daylight approached and we were thankful the Japanese had not chosen to make their counter-attack during the night. They had truly missed their opportunity. Now it was our turn! The night was not quiet and had not passed without incident. Many firefights erupted from every corner of the island.

It was during these hours of darkness that we removed our wounded and brought to the beach many boats filled with supplies, mostly the exploding kind. Piled high along the pier were piles and piles of food and ammunition—both of which were in short supply.

The Japanese had zeroed in on the pier that second morning and a lot more Marines were put out of action. As was expected, a lot of "snafu" developed during those first 23 hours. (Snafu is a word for plenty bad mix up.) Radios were not working and the regular forms of communication were useless. We had counted on help from the First Battalion, Eighth Marine Regiment (which had been held in reserve), but because of the bad communications it wasn't until after daylight that Colonel Shoup got the order through to take the first Battalion Eighth ashore.

Coming in amid mortar fire, machine gun fire, anti-boat guns firing with pre-set explosive shells and the deadly accuracy of the "British Twin Vickers," which had been taken at the fall of Singapore by the Japanese and set precisely in position to cover a large area of the beach where the Marines had to cross, coming ashore was much more hazardous now than that first day had been. Even before the Higgens boats reached the reef, Japanese bullets and mortars started showering around and among them. My outfit, the Second Battalion, Second Regiment, along with the First Battalion, Tenth Artillary, were furiously attacking to the south and west, attempting to quiet the antiboat guns which were so very deadly. There was no way an infantryman, with only a rifle, could reach the anti-boat guns still in action on the old grounded freighter out in the lagoon.

Robert Sharrod, a war correspondent, who was on the same transport as I, "The Blue Fox," crouching on Red Beach Two, watched the First Battalion, Eighteenth Marines, come ashore and wrote in his notebook. "The machine guns continue to tear into the oncoming Marines. Within five minutes I see six men killed, but the others keep coming. One rifleman walks slowly ashore, his left arm a bloody mess from the shoulder down. The casualties become heavier. Within a few minutes I can count at least a hundred Marines lying on the flats."

An hour later, Sharrod wrote, "The Marines continue unloading from the Higgens boats, but fewer are walking ashore now. There are at least two hundred bodies which I do not see move at all on the dry flats or in the shallow water partially covering them. This is far worse, far worse, than yesterday."

Word had been flashed on the PBX: Help was on the way. The Sixth Regiment which had been in reserve was now committed. This was D Day Plus One (November 21, 1943) at 1655 hours (4:55 p.m.). Lt. Colonel Raymond Murry landed the Second Battalion, Sixth Regiment on the beaches of Bairiki, the atoll only three-fourths of a mile west of Betio, in the wake of Naval and air bombardment. There had been fifteen Jap soldiers on Bairiki who were manning two machine guns in a pillbox. These soldiers were "fried" in their emplacement by a lucky hit from a strafing plane which punctured a gas tank exploding it in a burst of flames just minutes before the men of the Sixth went ashore. Now the Sixth Marines were on shore and the Regimental Headquarters section was transferred to the beach.

95

It became clear a commitment had been made to complete the mission at all costs.

Meanwhile, a mission of the utmost urgency had just been planned by Marine Intelligence, with the men picked for the job busily readying themselves on the cold deck of the Transport, "U.S.S. Doyen."

It is a balmy evening and it is the First, Second and Third Platoon of the Second Tank Battalion who had been assigned the task.

In charge of the First Platoon is Lt. Marion Drake, a grammar school teacher in Paonia, Ohio only 18 months ago. His assistant, Sgt. Ed Brooks, was an old salt with fifteen years service. Their job was to land in rubber rafts behind enemy lines of the Tarawa Atoll under the cover of darkness and return with a most important package, a mission which could have a deciding impact on the success or failure of the battle on Betio, at that very moment in serious doubt.

Lt. Marions platoon was to leave the U.S.S. Doyen in a Higgens Boat, transfer to rubber rafts at the surf line, and with each man carrying a semi-automatic rifle, hunting knife, ammunition and two fragmentation hand grenades. They were to infiltrate the enemy lines, careful to avoid any contact with the enemy which would blow the covert assignment sky-high.

Darkness came and the U.S.S. Doyen moved from its position, out of reach of Japanese Shore batteries, to dangerously close within the perimiter of the fortified atoll, their only protection, a U.S. Naval Destroyer.

The scouts eagerly climbed aboard the Higgens Boat for the ride into the surf line where they would transfer to rubber rafts to carry them over the 1000 feet or coral and heavy surf. Although they had all studied maps and charts of the area before leaving New Zealand, they couldn't be certain they would all land on their assigned beach.

"The Mission," somewhere on that heavily occupied island chain was a Tarawa native who had served in the New Zealand Army during World War I achieving the rank of Sergeant. His knowledge of the Japanese defenses along with his ability to interpret them were badly needed for those plotting the battle strategy and it could be responsible for the saving of many lives. "Sergeant Joseph" was his name. The mission of the Second Tank Battalion was to find him and bring him to the battleship "Maryland," where Admiral Harry Hill, in charge of Naval

Operations and General Julian Smith, Commanding General of the Second Marine Division were anxiously awaiting to interrogate him.

The Higgens Boat glided slowly ashore, slowly so as to muffle the sound of the powerful diesel engines. Time stood still! After what seemed like a lifetime for them, the coxwain ordered in a soft voice, "Surf ahead, this is as far as I can go." The rolling surf could be heard pounding the beach and the coral reef fringing the island; land was about a half-mile ahead. Transferring to rubber rafts the Marines crouched low so as to not make a target and slowly slid to the beach. Even though the surf was exceptionally heavy, they could thank the training they had received on the New Zealand beaches for the problem free ride.

Through the moonless night images and shadows of palm trees and outlines of the beach appeared as willowy ghosts. It was indeed thankful there was no moon; they were sitting ducks and with more visibility it would have been a disaster.

The rubber rafts soon came to a grinding halt on the coral beach. The men quickly slid over the side and made their way to cover on the beach. They hid the rafts among the bushes and formed squads, leaving one man to guard the rafts. The mission began and within a few minutes Sgt. Price's squad observed the outline of a clearing between the palm trees. This proved to be a well-traveled path leading to and among the thatched huts of a native village. At one of the huts an elderly native was spotted slipping inside. Sgt. Price hurried to the opening and put his head inside whispering, "American Friend, American Friend." The Native emerged from the hut along with a younger native who thankfully spoke fluent English. A call went out for Lt. Drake, who quickly came and after exchanging amenities with the natives the urgent question which was the entire reason for the mission was asked, "Where can we find Sgt. Joseph?" Lt. Drake was quickly informed that Sgt. Joseph was living only two islands north, not a far distance as there is a causeway connecting all the isalnds of the Tarawa group with the exception of Betio and the distance from end to end is only about 25 miles.

When told of the mission, several of the natives volunteered to go for Sgt. Joseph. Meanwhile it was feared by some that a native may be friendly to the Japanese and endanger the entire operation. They needn't have worried, all the natives were loyal to the British. The rescue squad was instructed to keep clear of the path as it was well traveled by the Japanese.

After several hours, at about 2 a.m., the natives returned with their prize, "Sgt. Joseph." He was told what was expected and needed. Without hesitation, Sgt. Joseph agreed to the journey back to the Battleship "Maryland," to lend his expertise to the Admiral and General planning the operation. Moving quickly, Lt. Drakes' platoon returned to the beach, reclaimed their rafts and, with Sgt. Joseph, set out for the U.S. Maryland.

Upon reaching the reef Lt. Drake flashed a hooded light seaward as a signal for the coxwain of the Higgens Boat to come in and pick them up. While awaiting the Higgens boat, a body count was conducted. It was determined that one man was missing. He was thought to have been in Sgt. Weaver's raft, a guard who was left to watch the rafts on the beach. Due to the confusion and hurried departure he was not missed. After a hurried, or should I say frenzied, consultation with his squad leaders, Lt. Drake reluctantly told Sgt. Weaver, whom he considered the most resourceful, to return to the beach and retrieve the missing man. Sgt. Weavers only comment, "Is that an order?" To which Lt. Drake replied, "Yes." With that terse order and reply, Sgt. Weaver, along with his squad, turned around and headed back to the beach. They made the journey quickly and located the missing man immediately. He, "The guard," was sound asleep; sleeping among all the noise of the battle of the adjoining island of Betio. With the excitement of being in among the enemy and the pressure of it all, he was sleeping like a baby. The guard was uncermoniously awakened and with no lost motion reboarded the raft and hurriedly paddled for the open lagoon. During the fast trip the raft almost turned turtle several times, an easy task for a rubber raft. Meanwhile, several hours after leaving the beach, Lt. Drake delivered his prize cargo aboard the U.S. Maryland to complete the important rendevous.

As a result of that important and dangerous mission by nightfall of the 24th of November Betio was secured and the airfield was in use the following morning.

The young Marine left to guard who fell asleep was subsequently courtmartialed for, "Sleeping during a battle," and sentenced to serve time in Naval Prison.

Back on Betio all hell was flying. One scene which gave the men a sense of victory on the way was Colonel Shoup, Commanding Officer of the Second Marine Regiment, strutting about the beach with a pearl-handled western style revolver slung from his hip, (like in the old west facing a shootout.) The men Colonel Shoup faced, along with his men, did not fight in that manner. They were sneaky and it was tough digging them out.

We were told the reserves were now committed. It didn't mean we were being relieved; everyone was needed. We were only being supplied with some much needed help.

One close to all of us found peace that second day of bloody fighting. William Dean Hawkins, "Hawk," had rejected death time after time, even continuing to fight with serious wounds inflicted on that first day by a Japanese mortar shell.

William Dean Hawkins citation for posthumous award for the highest award, "The Medal of Honor," reads as follows: "At dawn on the following day, ("D" Plus One), First Lt. Hawkins returned to the dangerous mission of clearing the limited beachhead of Japanese resistance, personally initiating an assault on a hostile portion fortified by five enemy machine guns, and crawling forward in the face of withering fire, firing point blank into loopholes, and completed the destruction with grenades. Refusing to withdraw after being seriously wounded in the chest in this skirmish, he steadfastly carried the fight to the enemy, destroying three more pillboxes before he was caught in a burst of machine gun fire and mortally wounded. His relentless fighting spirit in the face of formidable opposition, and his exceptionally daring tactics were an inspiration to his comrades during the most crucial phase of the battle, and reflects the highest credit upon the United States Naval service. He gallantly gave his life for his country."

It was in his honor, when the last Jap was burned out of his hole on Tarawa, the airstrip was named "Hawkins Field."

The fighting on that second day was just as hectic as the first. I believe our lines were stronger and we did have some sort of communications and some of the wounded were receiving more help, and faster, than on that first day. Some actions and remarks made by some of the men in the heat of the battle expressed quite well the situation. One redhead from, you guessed it, Texas — Texas was well represented — walking with shoulders bowed, plunking every once in awhile at some sniper in a palm tree, summed it up by yelling at them in his southern twang, "You sons of bitches want to die for your country. I sure

Japanese bunker immediately after the battle in 1943. — Photo courtesy of the U.S. Marine Corps.

A Japanese concrete blockhouse on Betio. Note shell holes from 40 years ago. Same blockhouse as previous photo.

From atop an eight-inch Japanese rifle. Note the tip of the barrell blown off attesting to the marksman ship of the naval gunners.

101

Tarawa, Nov. 1943. Major "Jim" Crowe observes and directs action from his command post. — Marine Corps Defense Department photo.

as hell want to help you." Then, with every other shot he would shout, "Tojo eats s--t."

One great help to us on D Plus One, was the increased firepower. The destroyers came almost to the beach, firing point blank. Several Pack Howitzers were fired using delayed action fuses. This allowed for the penetration of the coconut log emplacements that were holding up so well. On that second day, out of 85 amtracs that started the invasion, only eighteen were left to limp back and forth bringing in supplies.

One veteran of the battle was "Siwash," a fighting, beer-drinking, pet duck who volunteered with the Second Division in New Zealand. Upon coming ashore the only record of his accomplishments was a blurb by one of the correspondents who reported that, "Siwash, immediately upon landing, engaged a Japanese red rooster in beak-to-beak combat." Siwash was reportedly wounded and was the recipient of the "Order of the Purple Heart." This, however, was never confirmed by the Second Regimental Headquarters.

On that second day, November 21, 1943, many more Marines were killed. But with all the death, it wasn't the hopeless situation that first day had been. We were now getting ammunition and water, yes water — sweet water.

Water was a major factor, with the heat and perspiration we lost a lot of body fluid during those bleak hours, and although we had landed with our canteens full of fresh water, it was soon gone. We were licking our parched, sunburned, scabby, half-raw lips, dotted with stubble peeking through the salt like corral encrusted on our faces. I looked through bloodshot eyes and saw the unloading of five gallon cans marked WATER. These welcome cannisters had arrived from the troopship, the Zeilin. Anxiously we took turns filling our canteens, then taking a big gulp, not prepared for what we had anxiously poured down our parched throats. Gagging and choking, we discovered to our horror the water was bitter and rancid; it was badly contaminated. It wasn't until a few hours later that the full realization hit us as to what had turned the sweet water into such a foul tasting liquid. All of the five-gallon cans had been ordered to be painted on the inside before being filled with that precious H20, and all of our canteens were filled to the brim with that bitter mixture. Worst of all, it was to be all we had for the next couple of days. The salty brine from the blue Pacific Ocean would, I believe, have tasted better. Then I remembered back to the time aboard ship when the second Lieutenant, thinking we had not enough to do, ordered the painting of the cans on the inside. Could it have been the Second Lieutenant was readying us for inspection instead of readying us for battle.

Most of us huddled in our meager cover, dreaming of cool, clear, sweet water — and what we would like to do with that officer — that 90 day wonder who had made conditions of the battle even more unbearable. Both dreams were intense as the battle and the heat continued without mercy.

The time — about 1800 (6 p.m. it is D Plus One), the battle of Tarawa. Word spread around the atoll — we are definately winning — why? Because the Jeeps are coming in down the pier with their 75mm self-propelled guns bouncing along almost leaving their hitches. Around the beach a cheer rang out as the arrival of the Jeeps meant to them that the area was secure. But it was not so, as they approached it was plainly visible they had not come ashore unscathed. There were holes' in their sides from Japanese sharp-shooters hiding in the palm trees and among the rubble along the beach.

The battle continued hot and heavy, but now we were receiving assistance from the Japanese themselves. Upon entering the

This concrete bunker still stands on Betio. In 1943 a well-placed "round" from a U.S. Naval Battery exploded inside blowing its top off. The bunker is now being used by the few British in the government as a handball court.

Bunker blown at the end of Betio, attesting to the bravery of those who gave their lives to complete the task.

"His death was not in vain." Marine First Lieutenant Alexander Bonnyman Jr., awarded the Congressional Medal of Honor Posthumously. —Photo courtesy of U.S. Marine Corps.

many pillboxes and shellholes, we found the disemboweled remains of Jap soldiers who, holding a grenade to their stomachs, or using their big toe to pull the trigger of their rifles with the muzzle in their mouths, chose to kill themselves before we Marines could oblige them.

The weather was beautiful. We were less than a hundred miles from the equator and the evenings were a little cool, but not cold. The days were something else. The sun continued to crack our skin; lips and noses looked like a two-by-four had been used to smash them in and heavy sandpaper to rub them raw. Then after a short number of hours the skin turned black. It was indeed a horrible sight, yet it was better than seeing the bloating bodies with their stomachs exploding in the hot sun and the yellow entrails coiling along the white sand. The stench was terrible. No one, unless there, could imagine the smell of it. Today, thirty-eight years later, I find myself catching a whiff of that stench whenever I close my eyes and think of that day so long ago.

On the morning of that third day, I awoke from a fitful and often interrupted sleep — I don't remember sleeping at all, but I know I must have as the night passed faster than the first night — I thanked God, first for protecting me during the night, and maybe at the same time, damned those who put me into such a place. My night had been spent in a shellhole alone, well — not really alone — I was with two dead Japs and I wasn't about to move them, too many had been wired with booby traps. The night before I had barely made it to the rim of the crater and jumped in — after a short skimish — I wasn't about to look for another shelter for the night. During the hours of darkness I had vivid memories of the sharp crack of the Japanese rifles and the star shells lighting up the sky as the Japanese again and again tried to retake the land they had lost. That was the night "Washing Machine Charlie," a lone Japanese plane with its engine whirring like the sound of a washing machine, dropped one bomb on our perimeter. The lone plane also dropped a bomb on the line held by the Japanese defenders, a rather even-steven affair. One other morning "Washing Machine Charlie" dropped bombs throughout the island, they did no visible damage however.

Those "damnable bunkers," they were so solidly built they could only be penetrated with the aid of large demolition charges.

This was now the time to clean out the pockets of resistance. The First Battalion of the Sixth Regiment made ready a sweep from Green Beach. They were to team with the First Battalion, Second Regiment along with the Second Battalion, Second Regiment (my proud organization). Lt. Jones was given the task of cleaning out a pocket of heavy resistance between their outfit and Red Beach One, where the line had drifted, leaving some of the enemy to inflict casualties from several positions.

The Sixth Marines faced light resistance at first, but as the Japs were pushed into a corner bordering the other side of the Second Battalion's line, furious firefights ensued causing many casualties. Luckily casualties were much lighter among the Sixth Marines even though they destroyed over two-hundred-fifty Japanese soldiers.

Meanwhile, the Second and Third Battalion of the Eighth Regiment wanted to expand their beachhead. But, in the perimeter of the Burns-Phillips pier they ran into great opposition. A steel pillbox made with reinforced concrete walls better than five feet thick and banked with sand was slowing down the advance. Major Henry P. Crowe called for and received assistance from his engineers who attacked and made a direct hit. It was one of the Japanese ammunition storehouses and the charge and explosion blew off the entire top. (On the trip back in 1979 I found this bunker being used for handball by some of the British men who were in Government there). For more than an hour a furious firefight exploded the area as the Marines edged forward inch by inch.

Meanwhile all over the small island sporadic shots were fired — both by the Japanese and by the Marines. It was easy to tell the difference between the Japanese 31 or Nambu machine gun and the sound made by the 30 cal. Gerand or 30 cal. B.A.R.'s the Marines carried. When the Japanese weapons were fired there echoed the noise of a quick, sharp retort, while the weapons of the Marines made a more powerful sound. Sound however had nothing to do with the damage either could bring. Both were equal in bestowing death — a quick death upon whomever appeared in the crosslines of the sights.

It was here another brave man was killed and in dying received the posthumous award of the "Congressional Medal of Honor." His name was First Lieutenant Alexander Bonnyman Jr., United States Marine Corps. Lt. Bonnyman, in civilian life, was a mine owner from New Mexico. Lt. Bonnyman crawled

The Generals review the battle — Inspecting Betio after the battle was over are Marine Major General Holland M. Smith, in command of all Gilbert forces (left), and Marine Major General Julian C. Smith, in direct command of the Second Marine Division which took Tarawa. —Marine Corps Defense Department photo.

up the steep sides of the bunker under heavy cross-fire with some of his platoon, the Assault Engineers. They used their flame throwers, dynamite and demolition charges and finally, reaching the top, held it under suicidal counter-attacks by the Japanese. As the Japs charged, Bonnyman fired his carbine in flagrant disregard of their weapons and numbers. He moved forward, driving off the enemy. In securing the hill, Bonnyman had received many bullets and went down within three feet of some of the Japanese he had stopped.

Lt. Bonnyman was credited with stopping the enemy allowing the Marines to sickle the enemy down when they counter-attacked with machine guns, grenades and 37mm cannisters. Then, to end the life of the bunker, waved in a tough and bearded bulldozer operator from the Third Battalion, Eighteenth Regiment (the Seabee Battalion) who sealed the entrance with sand and coral.

The Seabees! What an outfit! The Seabees had been streaming ashore since the morning of D Plus 2 bringing in their heavy equipment in big lighters and coming in over the reef. We couldn't believe what we were seeing: the Seabees driving their heavy equipment onto the airstrip — which was still crisscrossed by rifle fire — and filling up holes and smoothing out the bumps and hills for early use by our planes.

The Second Battalion, Eighth Regiment and the Third Battalion, Eighth Regiment kept up the fight and by nightfall they had fought across Betio to the eastern end of the airstrip. They then joined flank with the First Battalion, Sixth Regiment. At this time Betio was about ninety percent secure from Red Beach Three southeast to the sea and west to Green Beach.

One of the problems in advancing in all the directions was in keeping men supplied with water and ammunition. Another important ingredient was to have salt tablets. We were losing water so fast it was imperative we take salt to stop the dehydration process.

We had taken rations for one day when we left ship. I only remember eating the evening of the first day, lying in that shellhole with the tank "China Gal" as a companion. After that one meal the smell, and the excitement of just trying to stay alive, I don't remember eating until returning aboard ship three days following that meal alone next to my gal, "China Gal."

Author's note: It wasn't until my return to Betio in 1979 that I saw some of the fortifications we were up against in 1943. I understood then why they were so impregnable. The steel pillboxes, which were numerous, were in the shape of a pyramid and had slits for the Japs to see and fire from. They were made of three-eighths-inch steel plate inside and three-eights-inch steel plate outside with a space between that was filled with sand. Yes, a real solid piece of armor. I also visited and examined the bunkers which still stand as a monument to their strength. They are a labyrinth of passageways and thick walls with the covering on top in some places ten feet thick.

Although my first priority was to stay alive, with many of the other "Gung Ho" Marines, securing the island came first. Then, if you had anything left, you promised that to God — at least while the bullets were flying around and life was so insecure. Many Marines were souvenir hunters and spent as much time hunting souvenirs as searching for live Japs. The sergeant I am leaving his name out as I wouldn't want his family back home to know how their beloved was killed — was an old hand. He was leather-skinned and had seen service in China and used to tell us young "boots," as he called us, about the "Old Corps." Old Sarg was souvenir happy and with every charge there was a time for searching the bodies of the Japs for worthwhile objects. One object he treasured most and found many of were gold teeth, which were plentiful among the Japanese. He would use the butt of his rifle and smash the front jaw of the dead Jap — "an anesthetic" he called it — and remove all the gold teeth which he would put in a cloth bag that he carried with the top stuck over his belt. All went well until the day the island was declared secured and Old Sarg went on a spree in collecting gold teeth saying, "We may go off the gold standard and gold will be worth a lot someday and I want to get my share now." It was within sight of the end of the island and from about fifty feet in front where Old Sarg let out a yell, "Hey lookey, hey I found a gold mine." Evidently he had come across a dead Jap with a mouthful of gold teeth. Then we heard a KER-WUMPH! The gold mine had been booby trapped like a lot of other Japs we had come across during the fighting. Old Sarg was dead. No one wanted his gold as it spilled out over the white coral. He was left for the beach party who would be along soon to collect his body for proper disposal.

Gold at that time was about thirty-six dollars an ounce. No one would ever dream that it's value would increase by twenty times in the next thirty-five years but you can't spend it buried six feet under except for a little to pay for the ferry ride across the River Styx.

Major Lawrence Hays of the First Battalion, Eighth Regiment had enveloped the beach pocket and, even though surrounded, the Japs were still resisting. The pack howitzers from First Battalion, Tenth Regiment on Bairiki and the Second Battalion, Tenth Regiment on Betio gave excellent fire support for Jones and his push on the southern coast and had succeeded in keeping the Japs off balance on the tail end of the island. This was the afternoon that General Smith decided to move his command past ashore. During the trip the coxwain of the amtrac was wounded and General Smith and Brigadier General Thomas Burke made a difficult transfer on the reef.

This was the time for the Japs to counter attack which was a bad time for them, good for us. They had waited too long. If they had not waited so long the outcome may have been different.

Now Lt. Colonel Kenneth McLeod moved his Third Battalion, Sixth Regiment from the Green Beach easterly to join Second Battalion, Eighth Regiment and Third Battalion, Sixth Regiment which, by this time, had fought to the western end of the airstrip, but a pocket had remained between them and Green Beach. McLeod and his men cleared this pocket and then joined Jones and his troops. Then they all joined the Second Battalion, Second Regiment and the Third Battalion, Second Regiment making the island almost on the secure side with the exception of the tail of the island.

At this time it was estimated we had seven-thousand effective Marines on Betio. Counting was impossible as no one would hold still, but it was reasonable to assume that one-thousand Japanese still remained alive on the atoll.

These thousand Japs had to be dug out, one by one, from the rivetments, pillboxes, fortifications and shellholes. Many destroyed themselves and many wanted to take one of us with them as they were taught it was their ticket to Shinto heaven. A lot of the Marines found out when they jumped in a shellhole to claim a fancy sword, knife or other souvenir that the owner wasn't dead, only playing possum. What a surprise!

One of the largest "Banzi" charges came on the third day at about 0400 (or 2 a.m.) when over three-hundred frenzied, shrieking Japanese troops came charging between A and B Companies of the First Battalion, Sixth Regiment. The Marines fought valiantly. (Is there any other way for Marines to react?) The weight of the Japanese attack kept growing until Lt. Norman Thomas, acting commander of B Company, phoned Battalion headquarters on the P.B.X., "We are killing them as fast as they come at us, but we can't hold much longer; we need reinforcements." Jones sent the following message back, "You've got to hold." Somehow they held, receiving help from the First Howitzer Battalion, Tenth Regiment, which, with thanks to the keen eye of forward observer N.E. Milner, placed withering fire within seventy-five yards of the constantly pulsing Marine line. Meanwhile, in the lagoon, the U.S.S. Schroeder and the U.S.S. Sigbee poured salvo after salvo into the Japanese assembly areas.

It was to be a horrible hour, but they held, and after it was over they were all proud . . . they were Marines, weren't they?

There were many stories to tell of that battle and of the brave boys who became men during those long seventy-six hours.

It would not be possible for anyone to sum up the "Battle

of Tarawa" with just one story. Each and every United States Marine who lived through those seventy-six hours of hell would, if asked, tell his own personal story.

One tale I believe would be told often would be in praise of the Navy Corpsmen assigned to the Marine combat team to minister those wounded in battle. It may have been true that many were conscientious objectors and their reason for being in that branch of the service was they weren't under order to use guns.

I wish to state here with "emphasis" the name conscientious objector had nothing to do with their manhood, just their belief in God with a reverent desire to follow the Ten Commandments, particularly the one of "Thou shalt not kill."

We lovingly called the corpsman attached to our platoon "Doc." Doc unselfishly gave his life at Tarawa to help his boys. I clearly remember many conversations when Doc would reafirm his sincere feelings regarding the taking of a life, even in war. The incident which made the biggest impact occured while boarding the landing craft from the deck of the transport Zeilin. Doc was carrying an M-30 Caliber Carbine, as ordered by the Company Commander, but upon close examination of his weapon it was found to be unloaded and there was no ammunition on his person. His reaction when he found out we knew was, "I will follow orders to carry the weapon, but no one can make me use it," besides, he added, "I need the pockets in the bandelier (a place for carrying ammunition), for first aid supplies." Could there be any doubt of his sincerity and love for his fellow man.

Myself, and many of my fellow Marines can attest to the corpsmans extreme bravery under fire, completely disregarding their own safety while wading among heavy enemy fire carrying the wounded to safety then tending to their torn bodies. As a result of their bravery and skills, many United States Marines lived through the "Battle of Tarawa."

While researching records of the "Battle of Tarawa," I came upon an interesting report under "Equipment Expended, Medical." The report stated that, during those seventy-six hours of what seemed like an eternity to some and proved to be an eternity to others, over six-thousand units of blood plasma went ashore with some four-thousand units of blood plasma coming back in the veins of wounded Marines. Truly an astounding record which further attests to the abilities and dedication of

112

these remarkable men, the United States Naval Corpsmen.

Many of these unheralded heroes were themselves cut down in a war they didn't wish to fight in. The casualty records revealed two doctors, along with twenty-four Corpsmen were killed. Three others were reported missing and must be presumed dead. When the battle was over another fifty-two Corpsmen were to receive the "Purple Heart Award" for wounds they received in helping others.

I must also commend the Navy on another fact. Only minutes before the atoll was declared secure, a Navy carrier plane fishtailed around bulldozers which were still patching up the airstrip and made the first friendly landing on what was soon to be named Hawkins Field in tribute to Lt. Hawkins who also received the Congressional Medal of Honor for his heroism in capturing the atoll. A loud cheer went up from every part of the atoll. That was the reason we came to this God-forsaken place, wasn't it? To get an airstrip for our planes. Now we had it.

The carrier plane sat on the small strip for a short while as Seabees filled in a few more bomb craters, then zig-zagging down the small strip of land, it took gracefully to the air amid more cheering. You could even see a few smiles among the cracked faces of the rugged, ragged and proud United States Marines.

"Tarawa Lagoon, 1979." Child swinging from tree out over the water. This is one of the playthings of the children of Tarawa.

Looking across a native cemetery on Betio, Japanese bunker in background. Note damage to trees and shell holes in bunker.

114

CHAPTER VII

FROM OUT OF ITS TOMB

On this bright December day of 1979, I am walking across the old airplane runway once again. Instead of bomb craters, dead bodies and bulldozers, it is filled with vegetation. With one exception: a small area where nothing will grow. The natives have turned this hallowed ground into a basketball court and other recreation uses.

Once again I step into the river of time. Nothing, and yet everything has changed. Standing in the blistering heat of the central Pacific sun, I face the atoll of Betio head on. Somehow it doesn't seem so formidable this 14th day of December, 1979 as on those bleak days of November, 1943 when each grain of sand, bleached white before the landing, was soon to turn red with the blood of the conquerors and the conquered. Betio is now just a small dot of land in the now peaceful and calm Pacific Ocean.

How different are my recollections of this battlefield when I last was here in November, 1943. Then it had seemed so huge. Or maybe it was only the impact of war that made it appear so. The place expanded beyond all reason and reality by the fury of conflict. Yes, it was a fortress then; it is not a fortress now.

Before me is one half square mile of coral, sprinkled with palm trees, many still showing the scars of the naval bombardment and nicks of small arms fire, while others are still holding shells embedded in their trunks.

Spread throughout the island are huge concrete bunkers, their walls blackened by the heat and napalm residue of the flame throwers which have disappeared, but the holes still remain where the naval destroyers fired point blank from near shore. There are many pockmarks from the shells which bounced off the thick concrete sides of the bunkers. The smiling faces and happy sounds of children playing among the instruments of death of an era so long ago seem almost like it had been part of a movie I had seen. It is truly hard to believe anyone could survive what really happened. Although now a beautiful tropical, emerald green paradise, the true Betio has once again emerged — it is only the rusting, discarded weapons of war and my unrelenting memory that belie it's image of eternal paradise.

Bits and pieces of the carnage left from the fighting thirty-seven years ago on the Tarawa beaches.

All along the beaches are hulking scraps of that World War II battle. Landing craft lie wrecked near the shoreline where we became entangled in the enemy's wire traps. We came in to the west of the pier. Red Beach 2, it was called. Of the eighty seven landing craft that were to bring us ashore on the first wave, eight became entangled in these traps. Many more were disabled as they went back to get more troops and fifteen sank the minute they hit deep water.

Now I look at these mechanical skeletons as I would the stones in a cemetery. Each one seems to mark the finality of it all. It can be resolved but never forgotten. I can't help swelling inside and feeling the need to look up toward the gathering islanders calling out in the name of us all, to the memory of the 2nd Battalion, 2nd Regiment, 2nd Division, George Company of the United States Fighting Marines: "I have returned."

Instead, I clutch my camera bag and walk to the office of the local government. I have returned and I would like to think that the men who never left will know.

The gentleman I meet at the government office is a Gilbertese named Ras Berike. He is the senior assistant for Works and Public Utilities. Quite a title for such a small place. His constituency here numbers only eight thousand, but there

The reinforced concrete command post of the Japanese defending Tarawa, Gilbert Islands, against the onslaught of the Marines which was battered by our guns still stands though the Marines own the Island. An enemy tank is beside it. —Marine Corps Defense Department photo, 1943.

Japanese Command Post, "Bunker" heavily fortified in 1943. In 1979 it is a shell with honeycombed passageways, and walls and ceilings of five to ten feet thick, reinforced concrete. Note shell marks on bunker and shell scars on some of the palm trees. "If only they could talk."

is much to do. He is an extremely warm and friendly man and proves most helpful.

Everytime I meet somebody and they learn of my mission, I am treated in a very special manner. It is gratifying to know some still remember.

Mr. Berike is so interested that he calls the publisher of the local newspaper who promises to come to my hotel on Bikenibeau to interview me. He will make a ferry trip plus an eleven mile drive to my hotel. Quite a journey in these parts. I make a mental note to prepare some information for him.

I am finding that it is unusual for someone like me, a former Marine, to come back here. I am the only one anyone remembers who has returned for many years except for the Japanese. I am told that each year the Japanese government sends emissaries here to take the newly discovered remains of their countrymen back to the homeland. They consider them as heroes. After hearing this, I feel a special pride that I have come back to pay respects to my fallen comrades.

After talking to Mr. Berike, I decide to walk around the island for a while. Later I will take the bus they have here, actually a large window van with no glass in the windows, and tour the island more completely. You can ride all day on the bus for just ten cents.

As I walk, I meet many natives. Each of them gives me a great big "GI" smile and a "hewow." They are the most friendly and curious people I have ever seen. When I find some who can understand me and I them, they always want to hear about America. They never call our country the United States. It is always "America."

One group of islanders that can speak English tell me that they think our president, Mr. Carter, is a very fine man. Later I reason out why they probably feel that way. They are such a gentle and passive people that they relate to the President's christian ideals.

Finally the sun again overtakes me and I stop for some refreshment. I order a very different drink popular with the natives. It is called a toddy and what a drink! It is made from coconut nectar. When fresh, it is very soothing, but it tends to ferment quickly. After a few days, it still tastes heavenly, but it hits like the devil.

The culture here is fascinating. A person probably could spend a lifetime studying the legends and rituals of the islands.

The one road through the Tarawa Atoll. This atoll is so small the road is the only point above the ocean.

The toddy was one part of the culture I found delightful. There's a good story in its creation.

The drink requires the nectar, not the juice or milk, of the coconut. To get this, a tube must be inserted into the palm tree at the point where a coconut is just starting to bud. The sap that would normally nurture the growth of the coconut seeps down the tube and is collected in a cup. It is very similar to the gathering of maple syrup.

To get the tube into the palm, the tree must be climbed to the very top. The trees are tall and without branches. I don't know the ethnic background of the people that do the tree climbing, but they are a different breed. They are called "toddy boys" and they have a special physical adaption. All of their toes are the same length. Because their feet are straight across the front, this somehow enables them to scamper up the trees as easily as we would take a Sunday stroll. Each morning, very early, the toddy boys go up the trees to insert the nectar tubes.

And they sing.

The first time I heard it, I didn't know what to think. There came a loud, resonant and very beautiful song cascading down from the sky. Looking up, I could see these natives, silhouetted against the rising sun, chorusing from the tree tops. When I asked why these people were singing, I received two answers.

One native told me a romantic tale from the glory days of the tall ships. He said that sailors on those schooners, after a long journey, would climb high up in the masts. As they sighted their home shores, they would sing out loud and clear to their sweethearts. They would sing songs of love and home and, most of all, of their brave deeds. The people on shore would then know that they were safe and a joyous homecoming would be planned.

I thought that was a beautiful story. Unfortuantely, I asked another native about it and he told me a completely different tale.

The inhabitants of the islands live primarily in huts with no sides. Attached to these huts are outhouses which have sides but no roofs. In the early morning, the second native said, when many people are using their outhouses, the tree climbers sing to let them know there is somebody above them. Simple respect for the neighbor's privacy.

After I have refreshed myself, I go in search of the bus. I pass one house different from the rest; looking more westernized. A lady waves to me from the house and I walk over to meet her. She is from England. Kathy Stevenson. Her husband, Ken, is the island controller. They are staying at the house of the Chief Justice. We share a lime drink, not a toddy, and then she shows me how to catch the bus. It runs every ten minutes, which makes sense since there are only two and a half miles of road on the island and not all of it is used much.

I want to the ride the bus to the island cemetery but I can't make anybody understand me. I try "c-e-m-e-t-e-r-y" and "g-r-a-v-e-y-a-r-d" but all I get are blank looks. Finally I put my finger to my head as if I were holding a gun. I say, "bang" and drop my head as though dead. Still nobody understands. Finally I give up and just ride on the bus until I see grave markers. The bus stops and I get off.

Standing on an island in the central Pacific, a place I had been trying to return to for many years, I walk among the graves — the hot tropical sun beating overhead.

There are no stones marking these final resting places as there are no stones on a coral atoll. To take the place of stones some of the enterprising natives have used beer bottles neatly outlining the sacred plot of an ancester. It really is a nice cemetery. It is a quiet place.

Carefully I walk among the oddly marked graves, wondering what sort of markers are used to identify the graves of the Marines who died here. I know, for many of them, the coarse coral sand and the blue tropical sky are their only memorials.

I know that the Gilbertese believe that at death, the spirit leaves the body and travels upward to where the "god Kakaa" sits weaving nets — some of the spirits are captured, the worthy ones escape and return to the earth. I feel surrounded by many spirits.

As I walk from the graveyard there is a strange feeling of contrast that I am to experience again and again. From quiet reverie and deep personal reflection I am suddenly thrust into a world of laughter and innocence. Night to day.

Approaching the beach, I see many natives, smiling and happy as usual. Friendly people, living in the sun on this paradise in the Pacific. They are neither burdened by the pressures of

Standing in front of the Pilon marking the the 25th anniversary of the Tarawa Landing are (left to right) Peter Elvy, with U.N.; William Tonatake, businessman on Betio; Dyllis Condell, with U.N.; and a native helper.

world society nor haunted by the past. It is another world from the Betio I once endured. I leave my memories behind for a while as I walk among them. It is like a stroll through a forest, from shadows to open light, back and forth.

At the shoreline there is a wooden walkway extending out into the seas. At the very end, perched just above the gently rolling waves, there sits a small building. I walk out with camera in hand to take a picture. The natives all smile and chuckle. I join their laughter as I learn the building is an outhouse.

Suddenly it dawns on me: November 21, 1943. During the night, the enemy has crawled out to these outhouses and abandoned amtracs and Higgens boats. We are receiving fire from the front, the rear and hell. Even our own planes are straffing us. The cruisers come close to shore and fire broadside. Of all the thousands of tons of shells from Navy ships, I know of no accidents. They have excellent spotters. As I huddle, listening to the shells wobble overhead and the WHAMP WHAMP of mortars and the distinct sound of the Japanese Nambu machine gun, I almost disparingly feel "is there no place on this island safe?"

All of a sudden I hear a *put, put, put*. It is 1979 and it is the sound of a small motorcycle with a bare-footed, bare-chested native driving up the palm tree lined narrow road. He stops and in simple English asks me, "Where you go?" I tell him I am going to the village as I am getting a little hungry. He motions for me to get on behind him which I do, holding on. Away we go. If only my deputies could see me now! It is about one-half mile to the government barracks where he lets me off. I thank him the best I can and realize that, even though so much of civilization has passed them by, many, many have motorcycles. I can also state with authority that I was glad to get to my destination with the speed we went for more than one reason.

Looking around there are a few buildings, but I don't see any restaurant so I ask Mr. Ras Berike for assistance. I am advised there is one place where I may dine and he will take care of the small detail of notifying the owner a man is waiting to be fed. So I eat dinner at the only place in town, a Chinese restaurant. There is a one hour wait because meals are served by appointment only. My dinner is served on a huge platter — enough for three people. I usually dine with moderation but the day had caused my appetite to soar. I eat more than half. The bill is $2.10.

After the meal I walk toward the bar outside. Almost everything is outside. The weather here is always so gentle that there is no real need for protection from it. The same can be said for the people. They are, as my children would say, "very mellow."

As I pass, the natives smile at me and then shyly giggle. This reaction to my presence might make me feel self-conscious elsewhere. Here, I Know it is because I am a curiosity and the constant attention is actually flattering. I am, in fact, a celebrity; one of the only Marines to return to honor his comrades and their memory. Ah, my public!

One young man approaches me and says his name is Terry. He wants to take me home with him to meet his wife and children. Then he says we can go fishing.

I visit with him for a while. Then I explain that I am to meet some friends, but that I appreciate his generous offer. We leave each other smiling and waving.

The people I am to meet finally show up. One is a girl named Dillis, a dilly from New Zealand; a man named Peter Elvy, from Australia; and William S. Tonatake, who lives on the islands and asks me to call him Willy.

Peter and Dillis work for the United Nations, promoting handcraft among the natives. Willy is the General Manager of the Kiribati Co-op, the largest exporter-importer on the islands. Dillis is an excellent artist and helps the natives design their products for maximum salability. Evidently she does a good job. I am told that last year the inhabitants of this tiny atoll sold $15,000 worth of handcraft items to the outside world. When that figure is put in perspective with the economy it is very impressive. Tuna and whitefish, for example, sell for forty cents a pound and even imported beer is reasonable, just fifty five cents a can. Nature provides most of the necessities of life. It is a very enticing and easy going place.

My new friends offer to drive me around the island so I can take more pictures. I become a typical toursit for a time. A place on the very point of the island is called "Pig Village." There is no mystery as to the name. There are pigs, pigs and more pigs. All are kept in this one place and the entire atoll population takes care of them. Pigs are very popular in this part of the world. Some have the same status as the family dog back home, that is until they are eaten. The pig sties are made of materials long ago abandoned by the United States Marines.

Corrugated roofing, pieces from Higgens boats. Even the old Marsden matting used to make runways for the airfield is now part of Pig Village.

Later, Peter suggests that we visit the sight of the new sewer excavation. The big news is that an amphibious tractor from World War II has been uncovered and an attempt is being made to raise it out of its sandy tomb.

On the way I wonder if it could be the same one that brought me ashore in 1943. There were so few "alligators" available that they made many trips. There is no way for me to know if it is the same one but the thoughts of that landing persist. My throat feels dry — as dry as on that first day so long ago.

Betio, November 20, 1943: We made our way inland about seventy-five yards as darkness approached. At least some of us did. For almost twelve hours the savage enemy firepower steadily increased the toll of American dead.

Friday, December 14, 1979: With my new friends, Peter, Dillis and Willy, I have arrived at an excavation site on the island of Betio. It is just one of many small places of coral that make up the atoll called Tarawa, but the events that occurred here in 1943 have carved a place for it in history.

It was here that we fought the most fierce and concentrated battle of the Central Pacific in World War II. It was here that U.S. fighting men — more than twenty thousand of them in the total assault force — came together to meet the enemy face to face. There were young men and old. Some of them seemingly fearless and many certainly afraid but all of them linked by a common bond. They were Marines! Men of the Second Division, indomitable in battle and rich in heritage. They paid dearly to affirm that tradition. More than three thousand became casualties in that seventy-six hour seige.

As I stand here these long years later, I know that many new Marine recruits are told again and again of Tarawa. It is a part of their mutual soul. Still I cannot help but feel a sense of sadness. The men that will continue the Marine legacy will remember always, but many others have simply banished that event to the dusty annals of history and statistics. Perhaps it is inevitable.

I can only hope that my story and visit will cause some to re-examine those times and realize the strength of spirit and sacrifice that men have felt for their homes.

Here, at the excavation site, is a disturbing example of "how

What is left of an amphibious tank after thirty-six years in the elements.

Amtrac uncovered in 1979 with bodies of three. This is the highest it could be raised from its tomb with the equipment available.

soon we forget."

During the recent digging of a sewer trench, a landing craft had been uncovered. The amphibious alligator is sitting half-in and half-out of the ditch with armor-piercing shells still protruding from the front. Because of its massive weight and lack of proper equipment to lift it out, it crouches there pointing up toward the clear Pacific sky. In it's tilted posture, it resembles a lonely untended gravestone in the coral sand.

I am told that the remains of three Marines, still in full battle dress, have been found inside. This is then a monument; an unknown tomb far from home.

I will follow closely the disposition of these Marines. After thirty-six years they may soon rest in peace beneath the land they died to preserve.

Later, after I am driven back to the village area, I think that perhaps this whole island is a gigantic mausoleum with many men lying beneath the equatorial beaches. This thought is echoed by the Island Controller, Mr. Stevenson, who walks over to meet me as I stand looking across the now forbidding landscapes. He offers me a car and a guide for my next excursion on Sunday. As we walk along the shore, he says, "Even now we are probably walking over your dead buddies. I am sure the outside world doesn't know what you went through. It is only because I am in government here that I know a little of it. My hat is off to you."

I feel very proud that I have returned. I begin to understand what it means to try to tell the story of Tarawa.

Tarawa was a shared experience. It can be told in numbers and historic retrospect, but the actual account of those seventy-six hours is the private property of each of the thousands of men who endured it. My story will tell it as it was for me, but the whole of it can never be related. There are too many missing pieces.

After I return to Bairiki by ferry, I am driven the eleven miles to my hotel in the back of the island ambulance. It is actually a large converted carry-all, operated by the Ministry of Health, the island's biologist, a friend of Peter's who arranged the ride for me.

As we bounce along in the back, he tells me about the local hospital. It is a Catholic organization and the staff is composed of "nursing Sisters" who are very competent and do much good. A year before, there had been a cholera epidemic in which the sisters' aid had been invaluable. They also work with the leper colony located at the other end of the atoll.

The trip in the back of the ambulance, while not very comfortable, provided some lighter moments. There is not often a medical need for its use so it is run as a sort of government taxi. Each time we stop to either let somebody on or off, the natives quickly gather and cheer. It is really an occasion for them. Finally, after all the laughing dies down, we roll on until the next stop and another impromptu carnival. Eventually I reach the hotel and my own hero's welcome.

Once again I walk through the village taking pictures. It seems I will never tire of the friendly reception that always awaits. This is such a wonderful place to visit; I just wish it weren't so sticky. The rainfall has been reported to me at about 350 inches a year. Several Australians have told me it is really just half of that but I wonder. Yesterday, in a mere two hours, we had seven inches.

After my stroll I return to the hotel and pick up my laundry; one shirt, two pairs of pants, two shorts, three pairs of socks and a handkerchief. All washed and ironed. The bill is a "whomping" $1.55. What a great place!

Saturday, I have spent much of this day in my favorite way — walking among the natives. I have used a lot of film, especially with my Polaroid. The people are thrilled with pictures of themselves. This morning the two girls who make up my room posed shyly as I took their photo. As the picture developed in front of them, they laughed and clapped their hands. They kept coming back to the room every five or ten minutes to look at it. Finally I took one for each of them to keep.

This morning I had a humorous encounter with a local boy. As I left the hotel the young man, a long-legged fellow, came up to meet me. He had a great big smile and looked exactly like Alfred E. Neuman of Mad Magazine. With cupped hands, he offerd me the many small white fish he was holding. He was so eager to please, I wished I had a place to put the darned things.

I awoke this morning with my leg aching terribly. It had plagued me throughout the night and I spent much of my normal sleeping time thinking of a strange event that emerged on the flight here. The pain was a reminder of a sniper's bullet finding its mark on an island called Saipan.

On the airplane from Kwajelan to Guam I was seated next

to a young girl from Saipan who had been going to school in Oregon. She had studied medicine for six years and was returning to her home to minister in geriatrics for $1.25 an hour. She was a fine girl.

We talked for hours about Saipan and about the war. She was too young to have been a part of that time but her mother had told her a great deal about it.

I told her that I had been a part of the assault on Saipan in June 1944 and had landed by Garapan where the sugar beet factory was. That was where I was wounded. Then, like a script straight out of the "Twilight Zone," the girl told me the story of that assault as her mother had related it to her.

Her mother was only ten years old on that day and lived with the girls' grandmother and uncle just to the rear of the town of Garapan. The three — mother, uncle and grandmother — had taken refuge in a small gully, out of the lines of fire. Marines appeared above them and shouted down in Japanese for them to surrender, that they would be given food and water. It was difficult to understand the words because Japanese and Saipanese, while having the same roots, are different languages. Finally the natives understood and came up with hands raised. They were taken to a barbed wire enclosure and kept there for several weeks. Afer the island was secured, they were allowed to return to what was left of their homes.

I sat for a long time lost in memories after listening to her story. My mind raced back to June 24, 1944. I was on a patrol to feel out a perimeter of resistance. The place was called Garapan. Clearly I remember coming to the brink of a gully and looking down on some people hiding. There was an old woman and several children in my view. I stood and spoke to them in Japanese, "DO MA RAY ME ZOO YA TA BA MA NA OH AH GAY MA SO E SO GAY" (Come out. We will give you water and food.)

Suddenly I was swept from my feet. There was a burning sensation in my right leg. I had been shot. I pulled up my pant leg and saw a hole in the muscle, gushing blood. As I waited for stretcher bearers to carry me to safety, I could see the people from the gully being led away. There were the children I had seen and several adults.

Now, these many years later, I could not help but believe that among that unfortunate group of refugees had been the mother, grandmother and uncle.

Time moves like a stage play. It had opened against the violent backdrop of war-torn Saipan as a U.S. Marine and a frightened family began a tribal narrative that would be passed down from member to member. The curtain closes over thirty six years later.

The girl sits beside me as we streak through the night. Toward home for her and to something I cannot describe for myself. Her head rests against my shoulder in peaceful sleep. There is the smile of a Mona Lisa on her face.

The trip from the lines on Saipan to the hospital was charged with excitement. I was put on a stretcher and carried to a jeep where I was loaded on top and away we bounced to the hospital at Charicanoa. Past shells exploding, star shells lighting the skies, and noises unidentifiable. We passed a large ammo dump piled about twenty feet high and spread for about twenty-five square yards. There was a fire at one end where a Japanese shell had landed. If the dump had chose to explode at that moment I would have gotten to heaven much faster that evening but only thuds and pops were heard.

On arriving at the makeshift hospital — I wasn't there long enough to know what it once had been but it looked like a chicken coop — I was carried in and laid down against a wall with many others. A doctor came by examining each one and making remarks, not stopping too long, like "U.S. Army, name of person, shell shock, Army shell shock." Then, as he came to me, he said, "Oh, a Marine. A bad wound. Corpsman, here, take this man to operating immediately." I was bandaged and put in a bunk (Army cot).

I carried a samurai sword with me from the battle which I laid under my bunk and kept my rifle which I wouldn't let go of. I was told by the corpsman that the night before a Japanese had sneaked in and killed several wounded as they lay in their bunks. I did not sleep that night.

The next morning I was carried aboard an ambulance (field type) and to a hospital ship that was waiting in the harbor. Once aboard, I was asked if there was anything they could get for me. I remember asking for one thing: a head of lettuce. I will never forget how good it tasted with nothing on it.

Then, as I settled down, a doctor came to minister to the man in the next bed. His left leg had been blown off that first day of the landing and they had made a clean amputation halfway between his hip and knee. As the bandages were being removed I could see the stump. It was a mass of pus. Festering was fast in the tropics and a doctor with a corpsman's help was using swabs to clean out the pockets. I wince even now when I think of it and the pain telling in the voice of that poor man as he attempted to withstand the probing and digging.

I was sure I was on the way to the states but that was not to be. Again I was landed on Guadalcanal. At a rear eschelon field hospital built from Quonset huts where I was to receive medical treatment.

The Marine laying in the next bunk had taken a bullet through the stomach. A clean wound. It wasn't necessary to even open him up. It went in and came out.

On the doctor's rounds, he asked him how he felt. He replied, "Doc, please send me back to action. I want to get those sons-of-bitches that did this to me. I'm fine, hell, I'm a Marine." In two days he was on his way stateside.

I thought, "If it worked for him why not me?" I didn't have the same doctor but was sure they all felt the same. On my doctor's next round, I said, "Doctor, please send me back to Saipan so I can be with my buddies. I want to get those sons-of-bitches who did this to me." Two days later I was on my way back to Saipan, using a crutch to get around. I guess I wasn't too impressive.

In a little over a week of healing I was able to go on patrol on Saipan with the rest of my platoon. On my last patrol before leaving the island, we had walked through the desolate wreckage of houses and advanced toward the hills, carefully clearing the rubble war had left of any hidden japs and often, after thinking a spot was cleared, out would spring a Japanese shooting in his attempt to kill at least one more Marine and earn himself a place in Shinto Heaven.

We progressed from tree to tree, bush to bush, and cave to cave, finally coming to an area of many huge boulders. As acting squad leader I motioned my men to go to the left around a huge rock and I would go to the right. As I rounded the flank, I caught the unmistakable sound of a B.A.R. (Browning automatic rifle) that Miller had carried and handled with such expertise. Miller had gone over the top instead of around and had caught the Japanese in his sights, ready to bring death upon me, his 31mm rifle barrel resting on the rock and aimed at the spot where I soon would be emerging. Needless to say, Miller never received a raking over for not going around the boulder as ordered.

Once Saipan was secure, beer was a rationed item and the ration of two cans every other night just wasn't enough for a good buzz and we all, or most of us, wanted a good party. It had been quite a few months since our last one in Hawaii. The problem was where do we get the beer? At least enough for the night and the nights were long on Saipan.

P.F.C. Peterson, a young, redheaded innocent looking marine from the midwest with a penchant for devilment and a strong taste for beer had "found" several uniforms. The fact that they bore the stripes of Master Sergeant was noted with delight. One of the uniforms fit Peterson and we needed another innocent looking yet strong type so we asked Pvt. Dale.

Dale was a bible reading southern baptist with a heart of gold who wanted to reform everyone and yet would do anything if he thought it would help in his quest to get under your skin and maybe get another convert. We managed to talk him into it by telling him it was for the good of the army as they were getting too much to drink and if they had less it may be the turning point for them to see the light. And as I said before, he had a heart of solid gold and I think he felt it was a way to get to us more solid.

P.F.C. Peterson, Pvt. Dale and Cpl. Solen left together. I learned later Solen had already stolen — I mean acquired — an army truck and had it hid out. They dressed in the uniforms, drove to the beach area where the store house was and, with the authority that only a Master Sgt. can deliver, ordered the "Army truck" filled with beer. When they came back Peterson was still chuckling over the fact that "they loaded the beer." We all made short work unloading the cases of beer and the truck was driven to another area and abandoned where it would be found later, minus beer.

That was an evening never to be forgotten. We shared the beer with the rest of the company, which meant each man had over one case (twenty four bottles) all to himself. The next morning our C.O. held formation to announce that someone had commandeered over 200 cases of beer and wanted to know if any of us knew anything about it. Of course none of us had the slightest idea what he was talking about but that evening at beer call when our 2 cans of "ration beer" was passed out, a lot of the men just passed.

This is another day and another year. On this trip I often need to shake the cobwebs from my cluttered brain, telling myself over and over, "No, it wasn't a dream; it really happened."

I must clear my mind as I fall into a troubled sleep thinking of tomorrow and my interview with an important part of today's media.

Saturday, December 15, 1979: This afternoon I am interviewed at my hotel on Bekinebeau, an island of the Tarawa atoll group in the central Pacific. My interviewer, who works for a newspaper called The Atoll Pioneer, is a native of the islands. His name is Kabure Momo. He arrives on a small motorcycle and, like most of the islanders, is barefoot and full of questions.

I know that Mr. Momo has made quite a journey to see me for, with all due modesty, I am a big news story here. So I try to explain to him why I have returned. In doing so, I have again appreciated how difficult it is to convey the emotions and experiences that brought me to this point. Though it has been nearly forty years since my last "visit," there are still so many things that can only be felt. Often I have found myself in a rather confused state, lost in time, in a swirl of disjointed memories. The reasons for my presence here are because of what occurred here so I tell him some of the details of the Battle of Tarawa. He listens politely and will ultimately print my observations and say that I have come back to console myself. It is a small part of the truth.

Mr. Momo is interested not only in my mission but in America as well. When I give him an Eisenhower silver dollar as a souvenir, he examines it closely asking questions about each part of it. "What does E Pluribus Unum mean?"

I tell him it is Latin for "one of many." That it symbolizes the unity of the American people.

"This bell is for what reason?"

It is the Liberty Bell and it stands for the freedom America believes in."

His final question is for the identity of the man on the coin. I tell him it is Dwight D. Eisenhower, one of our presidents. His face lights up in recognition. He tells me he knows of "Ike" and admires him greatly but has never before seen his face.

The afternoon passes quickly and I feel good in talking with Mr. Momo. I present him with an old campaign button of my old days as sheriff, along with a brochure with my picture on it, telling him they are souvenirs of my first election back home. Thanking me gracefully, he says the picture from my brochure will be in the next edition along with my story and the pin he will wear every day to work.

Telling me the next issue of the "Pioneer" will be published shortly, he adds it is called a weekly but usually published only about every three weeks or so — or when there is enough news to fill it. This issue will be out on December 20 because there is "much news" — a very important man is on the island.

I felt honored and a little overwhelmed by his enthusiasm.

The paper is published after I leave the island. Mr. Momo is kind enough to send me several copies. After reading my intereview by Mr. Momo, I suddenly realize these natives are no different from any reporter on a metropolitan newspaper; they all use words to make the story sound better. Basically the story is correct but . . .

#1. I was a member of the U.S.M.C., not Navy, as stated.

#2. I was wounded in my right hand by shrapnel. It was on Saipan where I was shot in the right leg.

#3. Only 12 men reported back to duty in the next campaign, "Saipan", out of the original company strength of 150.

Otherwise, it is a good story and I am very proud of it.

The National Weekly of Kiribati

Atoll Pioneer

No 48   20 December 1979   10¢

DEMOCRAT

ROBERT R. TWITCHELL

Courses Offered by TTI in 1980

THE TARAWA Techni-
cal Institute will
be running two
specific program-
mes in Construct-
ion/Engineering
in 1980.

The courses
will be of two
weeks duration.

Participants
to the course will
be selected from
students living
Community High
Schools and indi-
viduals nominated
by the Island
Council on Island
Community High
Schools.

During 1980,
the Institute will

be teaching Commu-
nity High School
teachers on Tech-
nical subjects.

At the end of
December and the
beginning of Janu-
ary, the Institute
will carry out
selection to enter
Clerical, Carpen-
try and Joinery.

Later in the
year, the Institu-
te will also be
offering courses
in Plumbing and
General Construct-
ion work.

As part of its
Development Poli-
cy, a selection
of an advance
management training
modules will be
offered.

Early in Janu-
ary, it is hoped
that the official
openning of the
low cost modular
house be built at
the Tarawa Tech-
nical Institute
in the Department
of Appropriate
Technology.

The Return of a War Veteran

BY KABURE MOMO

EX-SERVICEMAN in
the US Marine,
BOB TWITCHELL was
in Tarawa for the
first time after
the Battle of
Tarawa in 1942.

Twitchell was
here to visit
Betio where one
of the blood took
battles in the
Pacific was
fought 37 years
back between US
Marines and the
Japanese.

"Betio he said
was devastated
during the war.

No houses or
buildings of any
kind was to be
seen except bunk-
ers, machine-guns,
attilery and so
on."

Twice, Twitchell
visited Betio to
console himself
after being on the
islet fighting
three whole days
before the Japs
were totally wiped
out.

Twitchell was
among the 150
navies of the 2nd
Division, 2nd Re-
giment, 2nd
Battalion G. Com-
pany sent ashore

by means of
ambhibious tract-
ors to pave way
for the rest of
the navies.

Mr. Twitchell
said their mission
was to bombard the
area since the
natives had evacu-
ated the islet,
and there were
only Japs occupy-
ing the place.

On the battle
front, Twitchell
got his right leg
shot but kept on
fighting, until
their victory
three days later.

Twelve out of
150 men survived.

Twitchell found
his coming back
very memorable
and commented;
"If only my people
could live in
harmony with the
kind of sincerity
you people, have,
there wouldn't
have been war."

Twitchell, 56
married with three
children, is now
General Contrator
Bellingham, WA,
USA.

He left today
after a one week
tour of South Tara-
wa.

Woman Stabbed

A WOMAN is now re-
covering in the
Tungaru Central
Hospital, Bikenibeu
after being stab-
bed in the neck,
during the week-
end.

Reliable sour-
ces, said the

woman was believed
to have been
stabbed by her own
brother, following
an argument.

Police had
arrested the man
and he is now help-
ing them in their
inquiries.

The coral sands of the lagoon at Betio, Tarawa.

CHAPTER VIII

RED BEACH — TODAY

I spend the evening of this day talking with my new friend Peter at the hotel diningroom. The place is really jumping due to the Island Commissioner, a huge man about six feet-six inches tall with a bald head and flowing white beard, who has arrived in flamboyant style. I am told he is a native but he must have a lot of English blood in him. With him is an entourage of about ten, mostly attractive native women. He orders several tables put together in a line and seats the women and a few men of his party with gallant elegance. Finally he sits down at the head of the line of tables, still towering above everybody and presides magnificently over the festivities.

All through the evening he deals in grand style, calling repeatedly for various wines and delicacies. He speaks loudly with expansive gestures and arm waving. It is almost as if I am on the Riviera and Cecil B. DeMille has arrived. It is a lot of fun to watch.

The waiters and waitresses bring Peter and me more Australian beer. We were going to bed but this is really something to see. The waiters serve with such a professional style it is hard to believe I am not back in San Francisco at the Top of the Mark, unless I open my eyes. These men and women who work here all have attended a special school on Fiji to qualify for their prestigious jobs. It is a job much sought after as they earn forty cents an hour and no tipping allowed.

As Peter and I sit drinking our beer and enjoying the surroundings, sudden darkness envelopes us. The diningroom is outside and the sunset has struck with the speed of a cobra. Neither of us speak as we look out over the lagoon and see the clouds, dark as velvet, like curtains in a theatre framing a small patch of red sky. As we watch, spellbound, the curtains — as I think of them, the illusion is so perfect — sharply close upon the last light. I very distinctly can hear an imaginary clap in my ear at their meeting one another and there is a darkness so total that I cannot see Peter sitting just a few feet from me. The entire performance has taken just a few minutes but I feel a sense of awe that may never be rivaled. It is without a doubt the most beautiful sight I have ever seen. Upon returning to the United States, I told a high school geology teacher about the sunset. He replied, "It must have been on the equator as that is the only place on earth where that phenomena occurs."

Later in my room I again have difficulty sleeping. My leg continues to ache and I wonder if the pain could be linked to the memories these past days have evoked. The "old war wound" is persistent here, almost as if my body, as well as my mind, feels the excitement and pressures of the many discoveries I have made. I again think of the three Marines found buried in the amphibious vehicle on Betio and decide, definitely, to find out about them and others like them.

Laying awake with the windows wide open to the warm tropical winds I can hear the insistent chirping of small island lizards. Their haunting songs continue until morning, sounding just different enough from the crickets back home to remind me of the distance I have journeyed. Before realizing how fast time moves I am bathed in sunlight and find I have slept at least for a while. Rising, tired but eager, I head for breakfast then back to that fortress, Betio.

Each time I take the ferry from Bairiki to Betio I am lost in thought and memories. Memories of another ride in that same lagoon. Loooking over the light green waters of the lagoon, it is hard to imagine all of the dangerous coral reefs which hold the water in. It is almost like a huge lake. There is only one opening in the reef and it was there that our amtracs and Higgens boats came into the lagoon from the Pacific Ocean. Had that channel been blocked the "Battle of Tarawa" may have had a different ending. We pass many native fishermen in their "coolie hats" and small boats, busily engaged in "bring home the bacon."

Entering Betio's harbor and coming along the new pier, I can see Mr. Stevenson and his wife waiting. Mr. Stevenson is the Island Controller, which means he is the person in charge of communications for his government in a specified area which, in this case, covers about one million square miles, almost all of it ocean. Mr. Stevenson had previously had an assignment from the British government in Rhodesia, South Africa. His assistant is a young Scot named Gary Davis. Gary had been in the British military fighting in northern Ireland previous to his assignment. Both seem to enjoy their present posts.

Davis is a history buff and has studied the Battle of Tarawa

138

but tells me there are some missing pieces in his investigation. Perhaps I would help fill him in? I agree and we walk around the island, talking and making marks on a map he has drawn.

As we come to the point on the beach where the pier had stood I wade out into the water. It is warm; like a bath. Soon I am nearly waist deep. Beside me are the rotting supports that are all that is left of the main pier on "Red Beach 2."

My eyes are wide open, yet I can now see the pier with flashes from machine gun fire streaking beneath it. I quickly look to the beach and see a Japanese gun silhouetted against the sky. There is no Gary. There is no 1979. There is only war and I can hear the chaotic shattering sounds of battle around me. I see my comrades beside me, wading through the gunfire. I rush through the surf, eyes darting, and sag against the remains of a Higgens boat. Tears are streaming down my face. I shake my head repeatedly to bring myself back.

Gary is beside me and the boat I lean upon is a rusted hulk. It was not a dream; it is something I cannot explain.

Gary and I walk away from the beach and I am very introspective. So much so that Gary finally says to me, "I would have known that you were an influential man as you are intelligently quiet."

I thank him but say that I have been lost in thought, that I cannot help thinking of different people I had known on this place. I tell him about some of them and what I remember of their actions because he is interested not only in places and events but states of mind. As we move through the palm trees I suddenly recall a tall redheaded Texan that had fought beside me. I describe him to Gary.

His name was Adrian Strange and the name really fit him. In fact, nothing you could say about him would be overdone. He was one big, tall, redheaded, crazy guy.

It was near here, I tell Gary, that we were lying in the sand. We had just landed and there were palm trees ahead of us. Adrian looked up at them and pointed. "See that palm?" Then he licked his thumb — he always did that before he shot, like some moutainman marksman — and touched the thumb to his rifle sight. BANG! The shot merged with the symphony of mortar and heavy gunfire. A sniper fell from the tree. I hadn't even known he was there. Adrian was quite a guy. All Texan.

Gary asked me if Strange had survived the battle and I answered, "Yes." As we would move inland, he would constantly

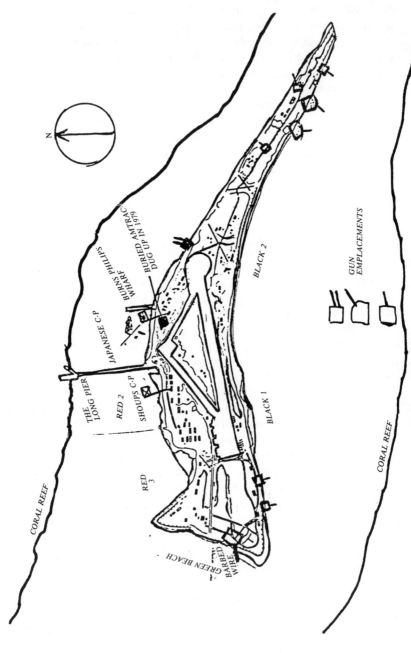

N

CORAL REEF

CORAL REEF

THE PIER
LONG PIER

JAPANESE C-P

BURNS PHILIPS
WHARF

BURIED AMTRAC
DUG UP IN 1979

RED 2

SHOUPS C-P

RED
3

GREEN BEACH

BARBED
WIRE

BLACK 2

BLACK 1

GUN
EMPLACEMENTS

CORAL REEF

Map of Japanese defenses drawn as the author tours the island with Gary.

look around him and yell in his high-pitched twang, extremely imaginative obscenities concerning the enemy. He would shout in American, not Japanese, but evidently many understood. They would spring from hiding only to fall as Adrian would lick, touch and fire. He was a real survivor, that one.

As I talk to Gary, I find myself recalling many of my comrades that survived, as if I have had my fill, at least for a time, of death. I tell him that one Marine buddy, Milton Sloto, is now with the water department in Los Angeles. I had seen Sloto just a few years ago.

Gary is an easy man to talk to and I appreciate his quiet courtesy. At one point I stop and look off, lost in thought. Gary waits and does not intrude. Afterward, he tells me, "I could see that you were in a private place and I waited until you cleared inside."

Soon our walk takes us to a single palm tree where an old basketball net has been fastened. Around the net area is concrete, broken and overgrown with foliage. I look beyond the makeshift court and see a Maneaba, a native communal house. A swift shock surges through me as I realize where I stand. This field of grass, where children now play and people meet, is what remains of the enemy airfield we fought to secure through seventy-six hours of death and misery. It is an area just three hundred yards long and two hundred feet wide. We named it "Hawkins Field."

Gary stands to the side, silent, waiting.

It is Tuesday, December 18, 1979. I have spent the last few days commuting regularly from my hotel on Bikenibeau to the small islet of Betio on the Tarawa atoll. Soon I will be leaving this place to see Guadalcanal, another of the battlefields of the Pacific where I fought as a U.S. Marine.

The visits to Betio have been hard to explain. The sun has been harsh and unyielding as have the memories that keep rushing back to me. I feel now that the war, these battlefields, the total expeience of nearly forty years ago, have been kept in a dusty volume somewhere on a shelf in my mind.

Each step that I have taken on these beaches has been the turning of a page. Each glimpse of the changed and changing landscape and each encounter with the wonderful inhabitants has been a postscript.

Whatever horrors have haunted my sleep in those thirty odd years are now put in the open.

Today, as I knelt in a bunker on the beach and brushed my hand across the concrete ceiling, spent shells rolled out by the dozens. I picked several up to bring back with me. I knew what terrible machines of war had caused them to be deposited there and I will never forget those days, but neither will I dwell upon them in unconscious reveries. The memories will be of my own choosing and under my control.

It is a sense of peace that surrounds me.

Betio has been dealt with and I look with anticipation to my journey to Guadalcanal.

Beyond the deep personal satisfaction my stay on the Tarawa atoll has provided, there has been much fulfillment in the meeting of the local natives. I have come to envy these people who many might call uncivilized or simple. Their lifestyle is naturally not as filled with modern technology as ours, but that doesn't mean they are uncivilized. And although their ways are relaxed, their culture is anything but simple. The sense of honor and morality that fills their daily lives would make a puritan look like a barbarian. Some of their other customs that might appear risque to us are merely common sense to them.

The right and wrong of their ways depends upon the circumstances and point of view. They are fine, good, people and I liked them.

One of my new acquaintances, William Tonatake, Willy to his friends, has given me a great deal of information about his people. Today, as I depart from the ferry, he meets me in a small Datsun he has commandeered, and we go to talk over lunch.

Willy tells me that the children of these islands are really two years old when they are called one. This is because of the high infant mortality rate. A person must live one year to become a member of the community.

Willy also tells me that he was given to another family to be raised when he was six months old. His family felt he would get a more affluent upbringing in that manner. I learn that practice is quite common. If one family has many sons and another has none, the family with none may be given a boy to raise and help with the work.

This system assures that the children will be well taken care of. The economics of these islands can be harsh if there is no sharing.

Willy's mother worked as a housekeeper for his new family

and it was many years before he learned of her relationship to him.

Willy originally lived on Guadalcanal and tells me he will take care of finding people to help me when I get there.

The Gilbertese have a stern sense of correct behavior and, ironically enough, the only major crimes that usually occur are a direct result of western influence. For centuries the natives have been imbibing fermented coconut milk on a limited basis. When the sailors and merchants introduced new and varied liquors to the islands, those products caused many altercations, often violent. Other than this, the islands are relatively crime free.

The sense of spirit and religion that the natives have is deep and established. The missionaries have done much here. But many of the old ways still persist. Some of these beliefs are beautiful.

The Gilbertese believe that the head is directly linked to God, a temple for each man. For this reason, it is forbidden to touch the head of any of the inhabitants; that would be desecration of the temple.

In the past, there was much faith placed in magic and spells, but that has largely vanished. Perhaps that was because the spells were often unreliable. If a spell didn't work, it was assumed that the other person had stronger magic. If any evil or good fortune — depending on the spell — occurred, then the spell was given the credit.

The Gilbertese always seem to deal in a very literal and logical manner that is not at once obvious to western minds. Their cultures are deep-rooted in ancestry and are ultimately very complex. They are simple only in their basic love of life.

After another day of sight-seeing and being careful not to touch any of the natives heads, I sit down to a fine dinner at the hotel. Joining me are my new friends, Peter and Dillis, the English school teacher, his French wife and their three year old son. They extend an invitation, which I gladly accept, to visit the King George School where he teaches.

The diningroom is packed tonight due to the Christmas airplane run to the islands. A C 130 Army transport which had a flame-out last night was forced down here.

The story of how is one of today's dramas in the South Pacific, but so commonplace the news media seldom reports any of it. This event occurred just one week prior to Christmas Day, 1979.

An adventuresome pilot was ferrying a Cessna 180 from California to missionaries in Borneo. To make the long journey over water, the cabin was modified to hold extra fuel tanks. This threw the magnetic compass off and the Cessna pilot became lost with low fuel supply some place over the Christmas Islands. The pilot sent out an S.O.S. which was picked up by the crew from the United States Air Force on Guam. They radioed their Starlifter C 130 which was in the air and in the immediate area. Using modernistic electronic gear, the Starlifter crew made a fix on the Cessna and then directed the pilot to a safe landing on the Tarawa atoll, without coming close enough for visual sighting. The C 130 experienced a flameout which made it necessary for the crew to land at Tarawa also.

The twelve United States crewmen and the ferry pilot spent the night in the Otenti Hotel and bar bringing the compliment of the hotel to sixteen which included myself and two workers from the U.N. The resulting dozen unexpected guests, all American, caused a bit of rearranging, but the hotel staff took care of all in normal excellent fashion. It is a real party atmosphere.

Early the next morning, equipment from Guam arrived to start the U.S. Air Force Starlifter. The Cessna was refueled and took off for its rendezvous with the missionaries of Borneo.

I may add that, after filling the fuel tanks of the Cessna, almost a gallon more fuel was needed than what the tanks were made to hold. The ferry pilot had indeed come in on a wing and a prayer and, of course, with the assistance of the United States Air Force.

December 18th: I visit the school. It is named after King George V and has all English teachers. It was established in 1922. Children attend by age, not class. There are barracks where the children stay during the term.

Everybody treated me like a VIP. They had been hearing about me on the radio. Almost every hut on the island has a radio. A wireless station on every island is part of the network called Radio Tarawa. It broadcasts daily news and entertainment and is used at the various ministries to publicize their activities.

The school has a rich history. It was established in 1922 to provide education for those who would fill minor clerical and administrative posts in the government. It was mandatory that families send their children to classes. Many were reluctant to do this because they believed traditional skills were more important, but the law was the law.

The British did care and had similar concerns for the potential loss of native traditions and the education was basically of a limited village type. Now the education is on a much broader scale and the school is a good one.

I get a ride back to the hotel on the school bus and the phone rings just as I enter my room. Maurene Donegon, wife of the Minister of Education, tells me she had heard of my visit — also on the radio. She asks if she and her husband may meet me for a cocktail so they can hear my story. We set a time.

I finish dinner early and about 5 p.m., as arranged, the Donegons arrived. They are fascinated as I tell them of my experiences on Betio, now and in 1943. They tell me that in the six years they have lived here I am the only Marine to return, that they know of, who had actually been in on the assault. I hear this often and feel good about my return.

December 19th: My last day on the island. Mr. Stevenson calls for me in a lorry to take me to the airport at Bonriki. The sun beats down and the process of checking in is slow and miserable. Finally I am seated and we leave Betio. The pilot is good enough to fly over Betio so I can get a good picture.

Looking down on peaceful Betio atoll, words which I wrote that last time I was awaiting the Higgens boat to take me away flood my mind.

> *The ground is hot. Our throats are dry and water*
> *   is hard to find.*
> *Yet, onward we charge. Never backward. We*
> *   never seem to mind.*
> *In our hearts, we know we will win even though*
> *   the bombs burst low and the shells raise a*
> *   terrible din.*
>
> *The strong, the weak, the sick and meek*
> *Fighting and dying together, side by side.*
> *Victory is on the way if we can turn the tide.*
>
> *At last! The enemy is on the run. The Marines*
> *   landed and with roar of gun, the Japs take*
> *   cover;*

145

They know, when that great Eagle hovers
   overhead,
Their day is done.

No time to quit. No time for congratulations yet,
But we will keep them a running, you bet.
Tojo, never in all his wildest dreams, counted on
   the fighting United States Marines

To turn the tide on foreign soil.
No, he never gave thought anyone could be so
   loyal.

I wish I could finish it, but try as I did, never could I find the proper words to end this ballad, written on Betio, Tarawa atoll, as I awaited transportation to my ship from the beach red with blood after securing the island.

CHAPTER IX

HAUNTING MEMORIES

With many of the friends I made while on Tarawa who are traveling with me to Nauru, the trip is quickly over. Landing about 1 p.m., and learning from the last visit to Nauru, I hurriedly make a dash for the dining room to have lunch and receive a wonderful surprise. Fresh strawberries and fresh cherries on the menu. Today is Wednesday and it will be Saturday before my flight leaves for Guadalcanal. This time, however, I will have some friends to help me pass the time.

During breakfast the next morning, I receive news which greatly upsets me. Joning me for breakfast is Tony Falkland, the superintendent in charge of the sewer project on Betio where the bodies of the three United States Marines had been uncovered after being buried for over 36 years. Tony confides to me that when the amtrac was first discovered and the bodies removed he wrote to the Nimitz Foundation in Fredricksburg, Texas, of his find. One of the Marines was still wearing his dog tags and Tony thought the United States Government would want to know so they could do something about it. The foundation informed Mr. Falkland that they had contacted Washington, D.C. and word was soon received back to Tony to the effect the Government was no longer interested. It was a closed file.

We both spent a long time at breakfast trying to reconcile why such a cold attitude. I had a book listing the casualties of Betio and when we compared the name Tony Falkland took from the dog tags we found it entered as "killed in action." Yes, it was obvious he was indeed killed in action but his name should have been listed under "missing."

Mr. Falkland told me he had about a half dozen body remains of American Marines lying in a tent on Betio that no one would claim. He told me he, in all probability, would be the one to give them a decent burial.

Each year since the end of the war the Japanese return to Betio to claim the remains of their ancestors, which they return to Japan for what they call an "honorable burial," while our own lay on a faraway lump of coral in the central Pacific.

I promise to Tony and to myself, "I will do something about this dishonorable situation."

Leaving Tony, after my 15th cup of coffee, I return to my room and lay down, reflecting on another battle, a battle I was not able to finish nor was I able to visit on my return. It was a place called Saipan in the Mariana group of islands.

After Tarawa, Saipan looked to us like a huge continent with its seventy-two square miles of land against the one-half mile square postage stamp size of Betio. Saipan had almost every type of typography, from mountains to plains, caves to reefs, cities and hamlets. The reef was very similar to the one at Betio and needed to be succumbed before meeting the enemy face to face.

The taking of this island, Saipan, was to be accomplished with the use of every type of fighting skill and more, some only on the drawing board and unproved as yet. As the men in the Higgens boats and amtracs were racing for the beach, the United State Navy was cruising between the islands of Tinian and Saipan with battlewagons blasting salvos after salvos into the enemy defense, and all the while from shore return fire was taking its toll. During this time almost two hundred Navy dive bombers made their strike, one by one, on the city of Charon Canoa. At 0815, or 8:15 a.m., the first waves of amtracs started their run for the beach. They came in small groups with the shallow draft boats in immediate pursuit. As they neared the beach these specially converted L.C.I.'s fired rockets from the launchers creating a scene like "Star Wars," a movie which wasn't to be made for over thirty five years. At 0843, or 8:43 a.m., the first amtrac climbed up and over the reef. Now it was time for man against man and machine against machine. Object: "Secure the heavily defended beaches."

During the four days preceding D-day, the Navy ships and planes had poured round after round of hot lead onto the beaches and into the towns of Garapan and Charon Canoa. It was still to be the armor of "khaki shirt" worn by United States Marines that would protect him against enemy bullets.

Many on that first landing party were inductees, the first men drafted to serve in the United States Marine Corps. They showed under fire that it is the "Esprit de Corps" which is drilled into every recruit which makes him the man he proves to be in combat.

My mind is full of incidents of those first days on the island and the night of horror while we lay in fox holes. The next morning we counted twenty-seven Japanese tanks that had been knocked out during the night after running back and forth across our lines. They were so close you could hit them with your hand. Most of the tanks were knocked out by artillery fire from ships in the harbor which had excellent spotting from a Marine sitting on a stump smoking a big black cigar all night, giving directions to the ship's battery.

On that torn beach and the pock-marked plains of Saipan, the first day claimed 238 men killed from the 2nd Marine Division and 1,022 wounded and 315 missing. It was a day of rifle fire against artillery shells, the Japanese had closely marked off by grid each sector of the island and their mortar fire was devastating. The Japs had counter-attacked twice that first day only to be driven back and almost succeeded with the second attack when tanks were used. One of the tanks rumbled to within seventy-five yards of one command post before being destroyed by a bazooka.

It was an unseen enemy like most of the fighting we had encountered and digging them out was the task of the enlisted and non-coms who battled like the heroes each one is in my heart. Evacuation of the wounded was done quickly even as night fell. The hospital ships in the harbor were filling up fast.

Many of the commanders who directed superbly on Tarawa were to fall that first day from wounds. One name that comes to mind is Lt. Col. Miller. He was hit on the way in by mortar fire and a Jap grenade caught him between the feet stripping the flesh from his limbs. His command passed to the 3rd Battalion exec. officer Major Stanley Larsen.

In 2nd Battalion, 8th Regiment, Major Henry P. Crowe caught a bullet through his ribs and then, as if that wasn't enough, was hit by mortar shell fragments. Major Chamberlain assumed command and led 2/8 in a new flank attack.

Then Lieutenant Colonel Easley was hit and Major John Rentsch of Ohio assumed command with 3rd Battalion, 6th Regiment.

Within the first ten hours the 2nd Battalion, 6th Regiment had four commanders. Lieutenant Colonel Murray was wounded and evacuated. Then his executive officer, Major Howard Rice, my old commander on Tarawa, took over. Rice became a casualty and Lieutenant Colonel William Kengla, who had come ashore as an observer, took command but Kengla was called elsewhere and the battalion was given to Major Leroy Hunt, Jr.

Both combat teams were in the same trouble losing commanders. Leiutenant Colonel Hays was felled by shrapnel soon after his 1/8 battalion was committed. Out of seven battalions ashore only Jones, who headed 1st Battalion, 6th Regiment, and Lieutenant Colonel Guy Tannyhill of 1st Battalion, 29th Marines, escaped injury on that fateful D-day. I believe the fact the combat teams were able to function so well even with changing of the guard constantly, shows how well-trained the Marines are in their duties.

Although command had been constantly reshuffled due to casualties, the non-coms and platoon leaders suffered less the first day than commissioned officers. It was the darkness of the tropical night they were not looking forward to, believing it would be a time of terror with the Japanese trying to retake the ground they lost during the day. We were not disappointed. Many star shells and small counter-attacks kept us awake during the night but it was to be 2200, or 10 p.m., when the worst came. The Japs, with swords flashing — they even unfurled flags of the rising sun and a bugle sounding the Japanese version of "charge" — literally threw themselves into the Marines' lines. All at once the night lit brightly. The Navy had been alerted and sent many star shells into the black sky. With the illumination provided, the Japs came head on into the machine guns, bazookas, 37's, with cannister shot and rifles. They fell back in disarray. Our artillery came on strong and finished the job.

The enemy's morale received a lift at that time as their supreme commander of the entire island group, Admiral Chuchi Nagun, had received wonderful news which he passed on to his entire staff and they in turn passed it on to all Japanese that could be contacted by them. The big news: "The Japanese Imperial Fleet was coming at flank speed to destroy the United States troops on land and on the sea." They must, they were told, hold us on the southwestern beachhead and wait. The Japanese troops acted as though possessed with this good news and fought with the fury of lions, even forcing the Marines back some fifty yards. Our commanders called for five of our General Sherman tanks and once again these iron men and machines sent the Japanese forces in confusion.

It was about this time a Japanese marksman found me in his sights causing me to be evacuated for treatment.

I stand in reverence remembering a poem put together during the battles early in the war. Reciting these words to myself, I once again feel a sense of peace.

As the twilight shadows darken
And the sun sinks in the west,
All the toil of day is over
And that is the time I love the best.

Just to sit here by my fireside
As the shades of night draw nigh
Often makes me think and ponder
Of the day that just passed by.

Softly now there came a knocking
On the door outside my room.
Then a form took shape and entered.
There was silence in the gloom.

Tall and stately was his manner
And I understood with ease
For when he spoke the penetration of his voice
Struck me with its first but plaintive pleas.

Please, Son, I'm your uncle.
Spare a moment if you can.
Listen to my cry for freedom.
I'm your only Uncle Sam.

Yesterday, our peaceful nation
Without thought of fiendish foe
Paid the price of crucifixion
Like our savior long ago.

Yes, Son, I hoped I would never ask you
And I prayed with reverend vow,
And, though God is with us in our battle,
I need your help right now.

Tanks and planes are in one unit.
Ships and guns another one.
Take the side of perseverance.
Never falter in your task.

Give your all to Uncle Sammy.
Help to make our freedom last.

I learned from the conversations with many on this trip that on the Truk islands, and on others in that area, many jeeps, trucks and other military equipment after the war were bulldozed into huge trenches dug for that purpose. As the machinery toppled into their graves, they turned upside down, landing on their tops. In that position the oil from the pan drained throughout the engines, thereby preserving them. A few years later, when the military was short of parts, they dug up these skeletons and salvaged the motors which were in near perfect condition due to the oil throughout. I was told the Japanese scrap dealers salvaged the rest of the vehicles for the metals. It was also enlightening to me to find out that the machines of war, built to defeat the Japanese, had been picked clean from the beaches, jungles and hills of most of the islands in the Pacific. One exception is Betio in the Tarawa atoll. I hope the Japanese are never granted salvage rights to that tiny spot of "hallowed ground" which will stay forever in my memory and should remain as a memorial and reminder that those that were killed did not die in vain, "lest we forget."

As long as I can remember, I have always told my children I've never smoked pot, used any mind-distorting drugs or narcotics. Yet I may have without knowing what it was. Upon leaving Tarawa among some of the souvenirs I took were several packages of Japanese cigarettes. I did smoke at that time but the Japanese cigarette smelled so odd I didn't think I would light one up. That is until one night at Camp Tarawa in Hawaii.

During a beer-bust, I ran out of Lucky Strikes (my brand), had consumed a few beers and decided to try one of those cigarettes I had liberated from Tarawa. Lighting up, I took a few deep draws and settled down with a bottle of beer and my "smokes." Soon I began to grow and before I knew it, I had grown maybe one hundred feet tall. Tent city was way below me. I was a giant in a midget town. The men looked like little toy dolls playing on the ground. I was in a Lilliputian world.

Everything blacked out and I remembered nothing until awakening at dawn with the blood within my body boiling. One of the squad helped me to sick bay where my temperature registered one hundred and four degrees and the doctor had no idea what was the cause and I certainly didn't want to tell him I had smoked something that maybe was a narcotic; men had been court marshalled for less.

The doctor gave me some A.P.C.'s which was prescribed

for everything, and told me to drink plenty of water. The fever subsided in a couple of hours and I was back to normal. The cigarettes were thrown in with the trash and to this day I don't know what caused the ravings of the night, but I will never forget that time in fairyland.

Often I have wondered if this could have been the driving force behind the "Banzi' charges? We always had felt the Japanese soldier was high on something. How else could they charge into the hot machine gun and rifle fire, climbing over the bodies of those that fell in front and stacking up like cordwood until the last one was dead in his tracks?

It is Wednesday, December 19, 1979. The island of Nauru in the central Pacific.

For the second time within three weeks, I sit in my hotel to wait for transportation to a place of many memories. The first visit here I was on my way to Tarawa, that small series of islands where so many men died in World War II. Before that visit my mind was filled with anticipation and confused emotions, but now Tarawa is over and the lump in my throat is for part of my next journey: Guadalcanal.

It is a three-day wait for a flight to Guadalcanal and, though Nauru is a beautiful place, I feel stranded. I am eager to find the sense of peace and adventure on the next former battlefield which I had achieved on Tarawa.

At the beginning of this odyssey, my mind had felt like a flight of old rickety stairs. The memories of those war-torn days were the steps, shaky and fragile. As I climb, nearly forty years later, each level seems to become firm and balance is achieved.

Guadalcanal is the next step on my ladder.

As usual it is a terrible hot day. I have become used to the climate to some degree. My strength is still sapped but less quickly. However, my nose is a sight and resembles a peeled onion. The real joy of Nauru this time around is the excellent food and service, even if it is slow. Dinner is enjoyed with Mr. and Mrs. Ken Mueller and my friend from Betio, Mr. Stevenson. The meal starts with a seafood cocktail of prawns over four inches long. They are delicious and I could make an entire meal of them. The Chateaubriand is impossible to turn down and the steaks that are served to Mr. Stevenson and me are so large we must split one between us. The Muellers order one T-bone steak that covers one large plate and escargot (snails) to be divid-

Japanese honneymooners in front of the Hotel Naurau, 1979.

ed between them.

The Muellers are interesting people. They hail from California but now run the huge rice field on Guadalcanal which is several thousands of acres in size.

Time passes slowly but I spend much time in thinking of Guadalcanal and playing cribbage with Ken. Ken is an excellent player but I manage to hold my own even with the memories constantly jamming my mind.

Cribbage, reveries and food. The routine continues and as the time approaches for my flight to that lush tropical island that has become a legend for the Marines, I have my own "Guadalcanal diary." I look forward to getting my thoughts in order so I can put them down on paper.

Thursday, December 20th: Dinner tonight is very special and exotic. The Muellers and I have raw octopus, tempura and sukiyaki. The octopus is excellent, something I would have never believed. It tastes fishy but with the texture of crab meat. Sitting at the table is a young Japanese man and his new bride. She is only four feet-six inches in height and very delicate, almost like a porcelain doll. Her feet are so tiny — they can't be over four inches in length. The couple does not speak English and my Japanese vocabulary, learned during the war, does not include table talk. Somehow we all manage to communicate. The Japanese gentleman shows me how to use chopsticks properly and even takes over the chef's duties cooking the sukiyaki at the table. I find myself again realizing how many years have passed. It is a pleasant evening and meal.

After dinner the Muellers and I go to my room and talk and play my favorite game, cribbage. The room has a veranda and overlooks the patio. We sit enjoying the beautiful scenery at dusk. As the sun sets in this part of the world Mother Nature makes a real production of it.

A native band shows up and begins tuning their instruments on the patio below us. They soon begin to play and sing and the place is quickly filled with people from the village. There is much dancing and laughter drifting up to our ears.

The natives are really restless tonight.

The music is sort of rock and the hotel manager asks us to come down and join in. We politely decline, telling him we are enjoying watching the festivities. About 1 a.m. the band stops abruptly, the instruments are taken inside and, as the last native leaves the open patio, the rains come. The timing is perfect. It rains three inches in the next forty-five minutes.

Friday, December 21, 1979: I have a fascinating talk with the native bartender in the hotel lounge. His name is Frank and he lived there during the war. The island of Nauru and its neighbor Banaba were the first to be occupied by the Japanese.

Frank tells about the Americans arrival to the area. He says he remembers when the Marines attacked Tarawa. The U.S. Navy first attempted to shell the airfield. He spread his arms out to show how big the shells were. Frank told me, "Many rounds fell unexploded on the beach and when the Japanese saw them and their huge size, they were confused. They were about twice the size of any Japanese shell. This made the Japanese soldiers very frightened and they ran in panic about the island, yelling all the while, 'We are losing the war. We are losing the war'." Frank also told me the Americans sent a plane, loaded with bombs, over at the beginning of the assault of Tarawa. "But," he added, "they only blew up an empty house."

"The rest of the battle you know," Frank said softly, ordering a drink for the house which consists of only three of us. All evening I listen to stories of customs and tales handed down from father to son and mother to daughter. This is an evening I will not soon forget.

Sleep comes easily and quickly for me that night. Maybe it is the Australian beer, but as the days go by and my eyes see what my mind had envisioned for so many years, I feel a sense of peace.

It is Saturday. Today I awake early to continue my journey, but I have mentioned before, this place, Nauru is a s-l-o-w-l-y moving area. Breakfast with fresh, red ripe strawberries (in December!). Then another wait. Off to the airport. Wait some more, then finally the welcome words, "You may board now." The one road is again closed off while we taxi to the end of the field, turn around, race down the runway and lift into the warm sky for the next leg of my journey — Guadalcanal.

CHAPTER X

GUADALCANAL — HOME FOR CHRISTMAS

1942. The landing on Guadalcanal was uneventful with the exception of the twenty-six Japanese Torpedo planes that came in from every angle to straf and torpedo our ships. I thank God all of our gunners were in excellent shape that day. All twenty-six Japanese planes were brought down, none were left to return with their story.

All of us were so green, just neophytes — most of us were away from home for the first time in our young lives. We didn't even know enough to be scared — that would come soon enough. It was when the fighting became messier and the patrols more hairy and the snipers became more improved on their marksmanship that the men became more and more edgy.

Today is Saturday, December 22, 1979, just three days before Christmas. This will be my second Christmas on Guadalcanal. My first Christmas here was thirty-seven years ago. It was lonesome and filled with strange and dangerous events.

I could never forget "our Christmas tree." It really wasn't much of a tree — just a scrubby, wirey, twisted tropical shrub, with shells hanging from its branches along with empty "C" ration cans. There were even human bones which were picked up in the stream bed dangling among the other decorations. On top, and sitting at a jaunty angle, someone had set a Japanese skull — it really set off the tree. It may now sound a bit macabre but in that place and at that time somehow it all seemed proper.

It was about this time our first contact with the outside world came about — letters, battered and torn packages. Even some bills caught up with some of us. Clearly I can see my first package from home, smashed beyond recognition. Eagerly I opened it only to find what were once beautiful home-baked cookies that had been turned to thousands of crumbs, but tas-

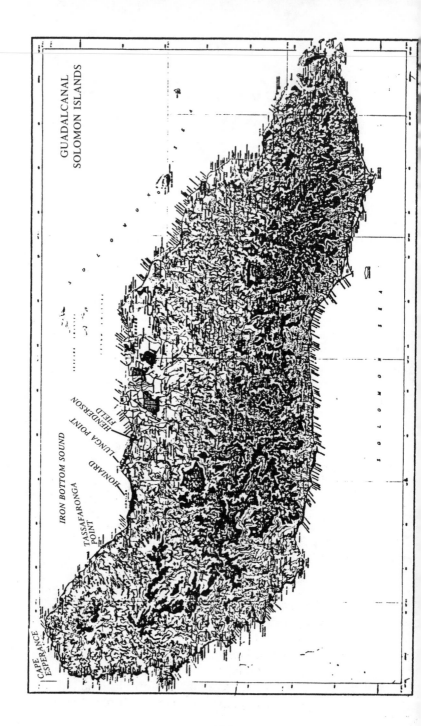

GUADALCANAL
SOLOMON ISLANDS

CAPE ESPERANCE
IRON BOTTOM SOUND
TASSAFARONGA POINT
KOLI POINT
LUNGA POINT
HENDERSON FIELD

SOLOMON SEA

ty crumbs. In among the crumbs were two cans of — guess what — Spam. Now I don't know the age of the reader, but spam-like meat was about all we had to eat in that God forsaken place, a food that many Marines can't stand even today.

Again I shake my head returning to the present but memories are slow to fade. I'm not on the ground, but we are only minutes away. Flying below the clouds, the green islands and blue water beckon me and I become more anxious. We wind among more islands and then all at once I see familiar sights — my throat tightens and my eyes widen. Pressing against the glass I look down at Tulagi and the Florida islands that lay below to my left (where President John F. Kennedy's P.T. boat 109 was headquartered in World War II). On my right is the island of Salvo, sticking up looking like Gibralter from the air, and directly below the straights, called Iron Bottom Sound, are the shadows of many ships and the boiling up of rust from their very innards as they continue to die, swallowed up by the blue Pacific Ocean.

Our plane swings in over the jungle and starts its glide path for the landing on Henderson Field, looking — almost staring — into the dark jungles. My mind quickly returns to December of 1942 and to a man I can't, nor do I want to, forget. It has huanted me these past thirty seven years.

Bronson was his real name. We always called him "Stud" and not without reason. Stud was a whiskey drinking, rough-talking Marine who had really been around. He was much older than most of us. I would judge him to be about twenty-seven or twenty-eight years old. Stud was always swearing, telling dirty stories and reminding us "youngsters" that he knew more about life and wild women than all of us put together, and perhaps it was so.

It was just a few days before Christmas of 1942. Each morning a squad from our platoon would take their turn making a patrol into the jungles in front of Bloody Ridge. This morning it was the turn of the Third Squad of which Stud and I were members. We had carefully made our way over two ridges, scouting the tops and sides well in front. We were in the middle of a heavily brushy draw when Sgt. Sloughter, our platoon leader, gave us the signal to deploy, take a rest and have dinner, our C-rations. This was to consist of one can of C-ration, about sixteen ounces, and several real hard crackers which had to feed the two of us. Stud and I shared this which was to be

"Salvo Island." Invasion craft and supply boats on the way to the beach of Guadalcanal about two miles away.

his last meal.

I was never what you would call religious, but then you will never find an atheist in a foxhole. I had been given an old testament by the Catholic chaplain on my arrival at Guadalcanal. The pages were well worn from my turning and re-reading each passage.

The night before this patrol Stud had joined me on watch and started asking me many questions about my belief in God. He asked me if he could borrow the small book he had been watching me read from so often. I felt good that Stud had feelings not unlike mine. Not much sleep was had by any of us that night. The star shells kept the night lit up most of the evening. I glanced often at Stud in his hole with the testament open and glad he was reading something besides trash with the help of the star shells and his flashlight.

Now it was another day and we were breaking bread together. Stud began asking many questions. This time about passages he had been reading. One question I shall never forget. He asked me, in such an innocent and quizzical way, "What does the passage mean that says 'Those that were first shall be last and those that are last shall be first'?" He went on, "Does that mean if I now believe, do I have a chance to go to heaven?" I tried to answer the best I could. I was only nineteen years old and not schooled in the word of God and all its wonderful meanings, but I replied, "Yes, I am sure it means if you truly believe in God you may be the last one to do so, yet you could still be the first one to enter the Kingdom of Heaven." I will always see that smile that came over his face as if all the troubles of the world had just left and he was truly at peace. He just nodded that he understood. Then came the crack of a Japanese rifle, a 31mm. It has an unmistakable sound. I watched helplessly as Stud pitched forward silently. He had been shot through the heart. He died instantly. There was no panic.

We all took evasive positions and a furious fire fight ensued. We fought our way back to our lines with Stud wrapped in a poncho. There were no other casualties. I could not help but believe that Stud was up there in heaven directing the enemy's bullets away from doing any further damage that day.

Our plane hits the runway at Henderson Field. I am jolted back to the present. Henderson was the scene of heavy activity in 1942. The constant hurried repair of too few fighter planes damaged through action and worn with heavy usage. Those pilots may have been cocky but they were all real gung-ho

"Gruman Wildcat" saw plenty of action in the later days of 1942 and early days of 1943 before crashing in a coconut palm orchard and brought to Fred Kona's museum. This plane could be the Wildcat flown by Captain John Smith.

heroes. They had to be sure of themselves. And what a workout those pilots of 1942 had in keeping the skies clear of Japanese aircraft.

Almost everyday at 10 a.m., you could set your watch by it if you had one which worked, several Japanese fighter planes or a flight of light bombers, would come in low out of the mountains to straf and bomb the field. I must give credit to all those early pilots with their "macho." One I especially think of today is United States Marine Captain John Smith (his real name). At 9:45 a.m. he would sit in his Gruman Fighter on the end of the runway and wait. As the Japanese planes came over to make their pass, he would gun the old plane and take off right in the middle of the Japanese formation. What a man!

About the middle of November of 1942, our company was bivouacked in the palm tree orchard between the airfield and the beach. This time when Captain Smith made his climb out of the field to join in harrassing the Japanese, his motor conked out. Many tops of the palms were cut out that day by the plane as it came to rest just a few hundred feet away from us. By the time we got to him, he was out of the plane and lying on the ground about fifty feet away. The sirens soon began their wailing and a jeep came tearing up from the airfield. We all felt relieved thinking the pilot was getting immediate help. We didn't count on what happened next. The men in the jeep went immediately to the downed airplane and removed several instruments from the cockpit. Then, sirens screaming, returned to the field. Another hour passed before an ambulance arrived to take the downed pilot away. I learned in those days that men were more expendable than airplanes.

It is again 1979. My plane taxies to the apron in front of the small airport building. We depart to incur another long customs check and the full realization "I have returned."

Starting out the door after customs finishes giving my baggage the once over, a native rushes over to me waving a single sheet of paper in his hand and saying in his best pronunciation of Twitchell, "Is you Tee-shell?" I glanced at the paper he carried. I read "Robert R. Twitchell." I nodded my head yes and answering at the same time. He asked me to follow him with words, "Come me." Outside a bus was waiting to take me to accommodations made for me before leaving the states, a place called Tambea Village.

As we depart Henderson Field, I glance to the west. There,

162

still standing, is that clump of palm trees that in 1942 was known as M.O.B. Hospital. Just a lot of tents strung along the grass with many trenches criss-crossing for quick cover during the frequent bombing raids. I spent a long week at that spot in January of 1942, suffering from yellow jaundice and malaria and, of course, dysentary. It was entirely possible, I know, to have a B.M. while dressed and the fluid traveling with such force it went through your pants without stopping. It seems almost unbelievable now.

One memory of events of that time is not pleasant. It is of Barney Ross, a hero back home, but to those that knew, he was not fit to wear the emblem of the United States Marines. I even now see him sniveling and hear him pleading for narcotics and for a ride back home when nothing was the matter with him except he lost this guts. When I returned to the states, three years later, and heard of what a hero they had made of Barney Ross, my stomach churned and my head pounded. I was close to becoming violently ill. But that was another year. I have not come back to tear open old wounds, but to close them.

I ask the driver tens of hundreds of questions as we drive those 30 miles to where I am to spend the night. He patiently answers every one even if he uses pidgeon English most of the time and I have to ask him to repeat more than once. Crossing a bridge, a spark is rekindled as the driver tells me it is a new bridge built to replace the old one at the Matanikau River, the scene of many bloody battles. I ask the driver to stop while I clear my memory. The river is now the color of clay, peacefully winding its way leaving small whirlpools spinning into the banks. Native children are playing in the shallows. It is now a peaceful sight; unlike thirty-seven years ago when the river ran red.

Our front lines were the banks of the Matanikau River. 37mm cannister shot protected our immediate front even though we had understood "cannister shot" had been forbidden by the Geneva Convention. I wonder if any war is fought by the rules. During the evening we would do a little swimming, mostly to wash the grime off that we earned during the day. It was pitch black. One evening I was out in the stream and brushed by what I thought was a log. The next morning I found out there had been alligators roaming up and down that night.

After several days on the bank of the river, we made an attack across, strengthening our lines and flanks, patrolling by

163

day and driving off the enemy by night.

A night deep in my memory is of standing watch. We all took turns. It was the month of November. Not a night passed that some fight didn't take place. This evening started out like all the rest. Our outposts were manned with 30 cal. water-cooled machines guns with the B.A.R.'s (Browning automatic rifles) on our flanks. Preparations were standard procedure, as any night the whole army of Japanese may come and we were prepared all the time. At times night patrols would be out in the jungles, but we would get the word where and when they would return. Also a code word was used, which was changed frequently, like *Lolly, Lolo* — words with L. On this evening we had been told no patrols were out and to open fire on anything that moved in our perimeter.

In front, along the crest of the hill, we had strung barbed wire with empty ration cans to warn of attack as the nights were sometimes black as tar. It was just after midnight; we had changed watches. The cans banging against the wire gave the signal someone or something was coming. It was the order that the machine gunners were to open fire first and we were to wait

Guadalcanal — today a beautiful beach called "Tambea Village." Salvo Island is in the background.

with rifle fire until we actually saw or heard return fire. The three machine guns, with gunners at the ready, opened fire. Each was capable of firing six hundred fifty per minute bringing untold death and injuries on whomever was in the way. At just that exact second each machine gunner pulled his trigger of death. Only a few rounds were heard to fire from each before all three jammed giving just enough time for the patrol, which was made up of our men, to identify themselves and stop this impending carnage.

I will never forget the look of that Second Lieutenant who was leading the patrol when he came across our lines and was told what had happened or what had almost happened. The only words I heard from his mouth were, "Oh, M'God! . . ." Such an understatement!

Finally we arrive at the Tambea Village. It is made up of thatched huts with fleas and I immediately alienate my new neighbor.

She is from Australia and shares the bungalow I have been assigned to. Sort of a jungle duplex. My mood, as I meet her, is not exactly merry. The accommodations are not at all what I expected and I am miles from the places I want to see. The heat, insects and the fact that I can do nothing about moving until Monday, has made the day a trying one. When I speak of these frustrations to my bungalow neighbor, she takes an immediate dislike to me and snaps, "Well, there's nothing you can do about it, so why don't you just relax and enjoy it?" Right!

It is nearing dinner time as I wake from a much needed nap. The rest has made my outlook a little less bleak. Fatigue has overtaken me often on this journey but this is the first time I have been this uncomfortable and irritated.

With Tarawa behind me, a personal victory, I am eager to now tackle Guadalcanal. I think of the people and events of this place during World War II. The memories are very strong. They seem to draw me to them, making every obstacle larger than life.

Sitting on a bench just outside my bungalow, I stare into the jungle which is just a few feet away, and am certain I can see faint outlines moving as though playing tag with me. My imagination runs wild. It is again 1942 and I am standing guard waiting for the enemy to make a move. That must be the worst part of fighting a war; not knowing where or when the bullets will start flying. Living conditions are another high on my list

Old bridge across a portion of the Matanakow River.

Native homes now dot the old fighter strip on Guadalcanal.

— sleeping on the ground with no cover, cold rations and, I may add, so skimpy, too. Water was not hard to find. Many streams flowed from the hills of Guadalcanal to the sea but you may fill your canteen at one spot and trod upstream a few feet only to find a decomposing Jap half in and half out, adding to the flavoring of the swift flowing water.

During the time I spent here in 1942, the natives hid all their women back in the hills. They knew they weren't safe from the Japanese soldiers. A protective lot, these natives. They took care of their own making sure their families were not subject to atrocities some had already suffered.

The natives themselves proved helpful to us. Our battalion had about eighty of them at one time serving as scouts, litter bearers and advisers of the mountainous terrain. The native in charge, Sgt. Major Vousa, himself suffered extreme cruelty at the hands of the Japanese. He was bayonetted several times, the bayonet slicing completely through his body. He was left for dead. Major Vousa was responsible for many of his friends coming to the American side and helping us in the struggle. I have learned that Sgt. Major Jacob Vousa still lives in the

Amphibious tractor abandoned on Guadalcanal used for bringing in supplies late in 1943.

hills in his village and holds a place of high honor among his countrymen. Many United States Marines owe him their lives. I make plans to visit him. It will be a great honor for me.

Another place I will visit was called, in 1942, "Bloody Ridge." Our platoon spent three weeks at that spot engaging in sporadic fights against the Japanese soldiers. Now it is probably just a quiet grassy knoll overlooking the sea. It is necessary for me to see it that way so I can put one more volume of this story on the shelf.

As these many thoughts ramble through my mind, I decide it may be better for me to take my neighbor's advice and try to relax. It isn't hard; the ocean is so beautiful and the weather hot.

Dinner is served and it proves to be the beginning of a new point of view about this place, "Tambea Village." Dinner is at the longhouse which is more properly a feasting place than a dining area.

A whole pig is roasted "ala native" for the meal and there are dozens of native dishes to sample. The music is festive and the whole atmosphere is that of celebration. As I look around I see many native children, happy and adorable, sitting on the floor in front of the band.

An Australian couple ask me to their table and I spend a delightful two hours in good company and conversation. The advice to enjoy is easy to follow in this tropical carnival but almost impossible to comprehend as I later return to my room.

I sleep very poorly this night in my thatched-roof duplex. I am somewhat used to the heat and insects, but I am unprepared for the added irritant this place provides. Lizards! They are everywhere. Crawling up and down the walls and across the ceiling. The noise alone is enough to keep me awake, but they make certain by periodically making nipping runs at my toes. Many hours later I surrender and arise to take a cold shower and my malaria pills.

Sunday: Tomorrow I will go to Honiara, the capital of this island, and there start my tour of the places where I once fought for my country, and for my life.

As I endure the seemingly endless miseries of this village, I suddenly realize that Christmas is only two days away. I have been invited to dinner by my friends, the Muellers, so I won't be alone. But home now seems a million miles away.

As evening approaches, and the heat eases a little, I leave

my room to be among people. Soon I meet a young boy who will make a lasting impression on me.

His name is John Sae (pronounced See) and he lives in the village. He is eleven years old. Somehow John and I drift together and soon we are comrades. I spend the evening with him, talking and trying to answer the many questions he fires at me. John is a bright, handsome lad and I am immediately impressed by his respect and maturity. He takes me to meet his parents and then on a tour of the village, including the local piggery. We trade addresses at one point and I truly believe that John will keep his promise to write to me. I know I will write to him.

John tells me he wants to be a doctor. Now his plans include coming to America to see me. When I tell him that I will be leaving the village tomorrow, he pleads with me to take him along. He says I need him to take care of me.

Later in the evening when I have eaten at the native barbecue, John appears to escort me back to my hut through the dark path. He was worried that I would get lost without his help. It is the last time I will see John before I leave and I give him an Eisenhower dollar to remember me by.

My dreams this night are a strange blend of war memories, lizards and a small, proud boy with large eyes.

Monday: Today is rather hectic. I move to the Mendana Hotel in Honiara after a long ride by truck. It is a beautiful place. The fact that there is no water at night because of a shortage doesn't even faze me.

I haven't seen a lizard since I got here.

Ken and Joyce Mueller, the people from California who now run the rice plantation here, come to take me to lunch and plan the next day. They will pick me up at 8 a.m. and I will spend Christmas with them.

The Muellers are two of the nicest people I have ever met. Gracious, generous and very interesting. I can hardly wait for tomorrow, due to them. With home still far away I feel the day will be one of the best ever, so far from home.

December 25, 1979, Christmas: I was right. This day is terrific. Ken Mueller takes me to the rice fields he oversees for a look around. We pass the old fighter strip now covered with native huts and scrub bushes. If only those daring pilots of yesteryear were here to witness the change. All along the roads we sight many old war relics and we spend the day trading stories and examing tools of war that have long ago become useless. At the Mueller home Christmas dinner is served complete with all the trimmings. The turkey weighs about eight pounds and had to be brought from Australia at a cost of a little more than seventeen dollars. After a delicious dinner, we go snorkeling in the beautiful, warm, clear Pacific. Sunburned, tired and supremely contented, we end the day visiting several Australian families at their homes. It has been a fine, fine day.

Today was unlike Christmas of 1942 here on Guadalcanal. That was just another day of patrol, another fire fight, another day of short rations.

Returning to the Hotel Mendana, I compose a letter to Senator Henry M. Jackson, a man I admire very much. I feel sure of his assistance in unraveling the mystery of the bodies found in the amphibious tank on Betio, Tarawa Atoll, that the officials in Washington, D.C. chose to ignore. I have borrowed a typewriter from the Muellers and sit up until late in the evening writing the letter for help. The letter is set out on the following page.

SEE "chap10 letter" *FOR SEN. JACKSON LETTER*

MENDANA HOTEL'S LTD.

MENDANA AVENUE   HONIARA   SOLOMON ISLANDS

P.O. Box 384   Cables 'MENDANA'   Phones 877/878   Telex 66315

Christmas Day   Dec. 25th 1979

Robert R. "BOB" Twitchell
5719 Cady Rd
Everett, Washington 98203

Honorable Henry M. Jackson
United States Senator
Washington, D.C.

Dear Scoop:

I am appalled at the callousness of some officials of the United States Government in observing the simple task of identifying and returning our dead heroes. Please let me explain. I am on a nostalgic trip to the Pacific islands where as a young United States Marine, I along with many others fought the Japanese in World War II.

I spent a week on Betio, "Tarawa," where on November 20, 1943 I stormed the beaches in the first wave with 2/2/2 G. Co. U.S.M.C. in an amphibian tractor. One of those very tractors was just unearthed by the company digging the sewer lines on Betio. The amtrack was in excellent condition and had inside it three Marines in full battle dress with rifles, helmets, etc. One of the Marines had on dog tags bearing the name of "ARTHUR D. SOMES." Mr. Somes was listed on the rolls as killed in action. Tony Falkland, boss of the sewer project informed me the Ministry at Betio contacted the Nimitz Foundation in Fredericksberg, Texas, who in turn said they contacted Washington D.C. The Ministry was informed no one was interested anymore.

The Japanese still come to the atoll "Betio," to return their ancestors. Are we so uncivilized and non-feeling to forget those who gave their lives for us? Mr. Falkland stated they dug up more American Marines than the three mentioned, but no one cares.

Well I care and if I know you, like I think I do, you certainly care. Please look into this matter.

Thanks for reading this and doing something about it.

Very truly yours,
BOB TWITCHELL

P.S. I am spending Christmas here on Guadalcanal as I did in 1942.

Wreckage of Corsair in Kona's museum on Guadalcanal. The shells are still in the belt, feeding into the gun chambers in the wings, and they are "live."

Japanese tank turret now in Fred Kona's museum along with Japanese anti-aircraft gun.

CHAPTER XI

OLD FRIENDS — TOGETHER AGAIN

Wednesday, December 26, 1979: Ken Mueller picks me up at the Madena Hotel at 7:30 a.m. Today is the day we are to visit Fred Kona's museum. It is a fascinating place, rich in nostalgia. Fred is a native who has built his village as a monument to World War II. It is about twenty miles from the capital, Honiara, and contains many wrecked airplanes, Japanese and American howitzers, parts of tanks and countless souvenirs from the war of Guadalcanal between the United States and Japan.

Fred Kona is personally responsible for the recovery of these war relics and is very emotionally moved when we meet. He was seven years of age when the island was under seige. As we are introduced, Fred grabs my hand, holds it tightly to his naked chest and sobs almost hysterically, repeating over and over, "God bless, God bless you, sir. You gave up so much for us. Too many of you died so we could be free. God bless, God bless."

I was very moved at his sincerity and found myself with misty eyes. Removing a Marine emblem, the globe and anchor, from my shirt — the insignia I had proudly worn back to the Guadalcanal battlefields — I presented Fred Kona with the emblem as a token of my feelings. Fred begans sobbing again almost uncontrollably. Between sobs he told me he would place my emblem in a place of honor, along with a plaque of my exploits. He then introduces me to his family who brings me gifts. Among the gifts are a watermelon and two pineapples. Fred has a jolly wife named Mary, a daughter named Mary and two sons, both strangely are named Fred.

Fred gives me a tour of his museum, proudly pointing out relics of airplanes, both Japanese and American. One plane, a Corsair, lies with its wings split exposing the 50 caliber guns still mounted in the wings with bandoliers of ammunition lying waiting for someone to pull the trigger so they can feed into the chamber.

One of the huts of Fred's museum is lined with Japanese

"Pistol Pete," was carted from hill to hill by the Japanese and used expertly against the Marines.

Fred Kona, his son, and motor from Japanese "Betty" bomber shot down in 1942. Kona Village, Guadalcanal.

174

Lockheed P38, "Lightning" in Fred Kona's Museum. It once was the king of the skies carrying a 20MM cannon plus three of the 4.5 caliber machine guns in the nose.

automatic weapons, another with the weapons of the United States Marines. Lined up in a grassy field are four Japanese howitzers poised with their barrels pointing skyward. The museum is indeed a tribute to those who fell in battle on the ridges and in the valleys of Guadalcanal.

Before I leave Fred and his memories, and mine also I might add, he asked me to write in his guest book that he has for visiting dignitaries. Fred insisted I write about the battles I participated in and when I told him it would take more than the one line most signers had used Fred smiled broadly, gave me a big hug, and said, "Please write about yourself, your battles, what you do in America." I carefully entered a few names I had remembered, "The Battle of the Metanakow," "Bloody Ridge," "Henderson Field," "Lunga Point," and, after filling four lines and feeling like a returned hereo, took leave of Fred and his very fine family. I told Fred I would try very hard to get him the bust of Franklin D. Roosevelt that he wants to put in a place of honor in his museum.

As I bid Fred goodbye he hugged me and sobbed again

Marketplace on Guadalcanal. Fruits look good but taste not like ours. Must be the nutrients in the soil.

almost hysterically, pleading for me to come again and, as I drive out of his village I am followed by waving of Fred, his wife, daughter and sons.

Ken told me that after all these years of Fred doing what he has done on his own, the Fred Kona Museum has finally been granted recognition and a few dollars from the new independent government of Guadalcanal. Fred deserves it.

Thursday, December 27, 1979: I spend much of this day walking through the native markets on Guadalcanal. It was just as you would expect; straight out of a Hollywood movie. Spread out over the ground are all manner of fruits, vegetables and wares for sale.

Even though I knew this island intimately from my time here during World War II, I still felt like a stranger. These happy people now enjoying their culture and commerce were nowhere to be seen when we Marines landed in 1942. Instead, there was danger and the enemy.

What inhabitants we did see were either pitiful refugees or brave men who fought with us to liberate the island from the Japanese. One of these men, Sergeant Major Vousa, is still alive and I have arranged to visit him tomorrow. He is a hero to his

Solomon Islands Clinic. Read the "Pidgeon English" on the window.

Main Street, Honiara, Guadalcanal. The island is 100 miles long and Honiara is the only city.

people and thinking of him makes the village scenes of today seem more unreal.

Today I am a tourist on a beautiful tropic paradise; tomorrow I will make the long journey back to remember the way Guadalcanal used to be.

As I stroll through the town of Honiara, I am aware of two men who are conspicuous by their western dress and appearance. The old cliche about it being a small world takes on a new meaning as we introduce ourselves and find we are all from Seattle, Washington. They are ferrying a yacht to Hawaii from the Philippines and have stopped here for supplies. They have been at sea for ten days and expect to reach their destination in another twenty days.

It is good for them they reached port here because last night a hurricane grazed this area and many ships were damaged as they were driven aground by the strong winds. Several large ships lay beached directly in front of the Mendena Hotel. One positive part of the storm is that there is no longer a water shortage on the island.

Friday, December 28, 1979: I awake early eager to see more

Bits and pieces of planes wrecked on Guadalcanal over forty years ago.

178

of this island at peace. A real treat was in store as I was able to take a leisurely shower; a big change from the past few days discomfort due to water rationing.

I arrange with the hotel for a car and a guide to take me to the outlying areas I am anxious to visit. It is a good thing I have a driver as the roads are incredibly primitive. The guide, a bulky native from the hotel, arrives. We are soon on our way. First stop, the Betikema Copper Company, a favorite tourist attraction. It is here the natives make hammered copper plaques and many artifacts and curios patterned after their culture. The Betikema Copper Company is also a Seventh Day Adventist School, a very interesting place. As a typical tourist, I purchase several souvenirs and ask that a special plaque be made for me and delivered to the hotel. As I am leaving the island a runner arrives delivering my order.

My mission today is very important to me, I can't wait to see Sergeant Major Vousa. Sergeant Vousa was the senior Police Officer or Chief of Police when the Japanese invaded on June 29, 1942. Sergeant Vousa being a conscientious officer and extremely protective of his constituency wanted to go arrest the

A view of the "Guadalcanal Yacht Club," from the harbor. Most of the visitors were from other islands and arrives in larger canoes.

invaders, but he was disuaded when it was learned of the over-whelming number of soldiers that had come ashore. Vousa had gone underground and waited for the Americans he was sure would come to rescue him and his people.

When the Marines landed, Vousa came down from the hills and was there to greet them and offer his valuable services. He was given a small flag of the United States which he carried tucked in his waist and would show as his safe passage through Marine lines. Sergeant Vousa made many scouting missions, one of which he was captured by the Japanese soldiers while on his way to Koli Point. They found his American flag which he proudly wore. He was relentlesly questioned on information concerning our outpost lines and perimeter. He steadfastly refused to tell the Japs anything. Angered by his refusal, they tied him to a tree with ropes and ran a bayonet through his body half a dozen times, one going through his throat, and left him for dead. Vousa, with superhuman effort, chewed through several strands of rope, tore them from his body and crawling on his hands and knees, left a trail of blood back to our lines. Even then Sergeant Vousa waved away medical help until he had briefed the intelligence unit of what he had seen on his scouting mission. He would say many times, "It was God's will."

Vousa also gave much credit to the Navy doctors for his miraculous recovery. General Vandergrift awarded him the "Silver Star" for his bravery, along with the rank of Sergeant Major in the United States Marine Corps. Sergeant Major Vousa was more proud of those awards than the honor bestowed upon him in 1979 by the Queen Mother, "Knighthood." He was "Sir Vousa."

Marines that were there and those that were to be Marines know of the deeds and sacrifices of Sergeant Vousa. Not only his direct help, but his assistance in recruiting the many others who came to our aid. Had it not been for these brave men the war would have been much more costly in lives.

A man's memory plays many tricks, remembering incidents and who the cast of characters were along with the dates, but I can place them on Guadalcanal in the early days of fighting in 1942. Our company had captured two Japanese soldiers during a patrol and we were holding them to be interrogated by intelligence who were to be in by morning. As we were in bivouac some of the natives who helped us in various duties volunteered to stand guard over these Japanese prisoners enabling us to get our much needed rest. We had been on an overnight patrol.

The Japs were tied to trees and the natives left on guard. That morning upon awakening we found one of the prisoners dead and the other visibly shaken, "scared out of his wits." We couldn't accuse the natives of brutality, but the fact was one prisoner was dead.

The natives requested permission to make up a burial party, request was granted. They drew a set of lines in the sand measuring close to the width and length of the men they were to bury and using cans scooped up sand within this outline about two feet deep. Deciding the hole was deep enough the four natives each took an arm and a leg. The natives were chanting as they tossed the man high in the air. He came down with a resounding plop, but alas, his arms were too wide and his legs too long. Borrowing a rifle one of the natives smashed the butt into each arm and leg, breaking and then gently folding these appendages within the perimeter of the hole they had scooped out. They then filled the top of the pit with open and empty ration cans and danced, pushing the sharp ends into the body. They then filled the rest of the grave with sand. Meantime, the Japanese who was still alive pleaded for mercy. He was soon taken to battalion headquarters for questioning and I have no knowledge of what occurred at his briefing.

I well remember Sgt. Vousa as I saw him last, a proud man with many American friends. I can't help wondering if he has changed as much as his land has.

We drive more than twelve miles in our small auto and as we pass the various areas the landscape evokes flashes of war sleeping still within me. The jungle-like terrain is dense and yet it is beautiful, once not so many years ago it was ominous.

After many turns the car makes a turn onto a path that at first appears almost impassable. Soon we are weaving our way through a maze of palm oil trees. The next five miles we are whipping in and around thick foliage until we are stopped by a field of tall grass. I follow the guide as we wade through the tall weeds towering over our heads, pushing them aside only to encounter another wall of grass, at last the final strands of grass separates and ahead is a lush green clearing near to the sea and surrounded by tall palms.

I have arrived at, "California Village." This is Sergeant Vousa's retreat, so named after returning from a trip to the United States. In the center of this amazing park is a tall flagpole. As I raise my eyes to the top a chill goes up and down my spine. Flying proudly is the stars and stripes, "Old Glory." Below the pole setting on a bench next to a plaque honoring Sgt. Vousa, "My Guadalcanal Hero," Sgt. Vousa sits smiling a hearty welcome.

I had not seen this man in over thirty-six years and yet it seemed like yesterday as we greeted each other and told lies about how little we had aged.

He is an amazing man and he wanted to know all about his old friends, the men he and I had fought beside in the war. There is much joy and deep sorrow in our meeting. His delight in my survival and mission to this place is great as is my feelings upon being here with, "the old scout," after so long a time had passed.

Emotions run the day as we laugh and cry in the same minute. When Vousa asks me about one special friend, "Sergeant Slaughter," I must tell him that he had died. He asks me if Sgt. Slaughter had been sick long before his death I tell him, "The Japanese killed him on the Tarawa invasion." Vousa gasps, "Oh, No!"

We talk for a long time and take many pictures before I

"Sir" Vousa in front of the plaque to his bravery and service in WWII.

182

leave him. As I depart he is waving to me from beneath his beloved flag.

"Sergeant Major Vousa," the brave old scout, passed away in 1984 and now lies buried in his jungle home which he named "California Village." His age, no one is sure, but his family is certain is over 90. Just shortly before his death he was invited to attend a reunion of Marine Veterans he fought with in Guadalcanal. He declined the invitation with this statement: Tell them I love them all, me old man now and me longer look good no more, but me never forget."

Nor will we, God bless and keep you unto Him.

It is several hours later when we finally return to the hotel, I hardly notice the return trip. The driver tells me we have traveled more than fifty miles, a long way in this jungle and then he tells me apologetically, "the fare will be very dear, nearly seven dollars." How wrong he is, there is no price to match this experience.

The next morning, Saturday I board a glass-bottomed boat

Just off the beach of Guadalcanal, the Hotel "Mendena" is in the background. The Japanese gentleman in the foreground is the Ambassador from New Guinea. His father was a Japanese soldier killed in the fighting on Guadalcanal.

Native children playing at the mouth of the Metanakow River, Guadalcanal, 1979. They were so helpful, turning our boat to go upstream.

for a sightseeing journey over the ocean bottom. It is meant to be a sightseeing tour of the coral formations and exotic tropical fish that inhabit here but I find much more interesting subjects which have lain on the ocean bottom for nearly forty years.

Our attention is called to an F-4-F Gruman Fighter Plane lying in 30-feet of water looking only an arms length away. We are told this plane fell to Japanese gunners at the start of the American Assault on August 7, 1942. The plane has been resting in that spot for over thirty-seven years. A couple of years back a diver brought up the dog tags of the pilot and his parents were notified of the find. They made the trip to Guadalcanal to see the tomb of their son. Only last year a driver, in checking the wreckage, found the tires to be filled with air as they were when it had crashed into the sea. I made a note of that fact, they are, "Michelin tires." When I returned to the United States my car will have Michelin Tires installed.

Family on the outskirts of Bloody Ridge, Guadalcanal. Note pig in arm. He, too, is a family member until time to butcher.

The guide is filled with many stories of the war and, when he is aware that I was a part of that war, he asks many questions. I find I am as much a point of interest as the scenery.

Sitting next to me in the glassbottomed boat is a young Japanese man. He tells me an interesting story. He said, "I was born in 1942, the same year of the Guadalcanal campaign. My father was a Japanese soldier in Burma and was killed in the fighting, even before I was born." As I lean close to him so I can understand more clearly what he is saying, the rest of the passengers seem all at once to turn their cameras on us. I would guess there are many places these pictures will turn up, for the other travelers are from all over the world. The real drama could never be captured on film.

Another war relic we stop over is a Japanese tank which is lying with just the tip of the turret breaking water. Then on to the mouth of the Matanikau River. The banks are lined with native huts and clotheslines showing brightly colored clothing hanging there to dry. Today it is a river of life for the natives. Yesterday it was a River of Death.

Today is Sunday, December 30, 1979. Church is where I

should be on this special day, but it is even more special as I hire a taxi and a native driver to take me to a place which holds many violent memories for me, "Bloody Ridge." As a Marine here in 1942, fighting for my very life, 37 years ago, that knoll, "Bloody Ridge" was home to me. For a period of three weeks my home was a cold foxhole, surrounded by the enemy, with almost impenetrable jungle in every direction, except up.

These fire fights continued endlessly, day after day, night after night. During the days we took turns on patrol driving the Japanese soldiers back into the hills and dense jungle. Each night they would silently creep out of their cover and attempt to overrun our positions. In the morning it was the same; drive them back again. It was what you could call a deadly version of "King of the Hill."

My taxi is an old Datsun with severe clutch problems and there are times when I feel I could get out and push faster than we are going up some of the hills. After what seemed like a long time, we arrived at a small village just on the edge of "Bloody Ridge." The village contained huts for three families, all related and all with many children. They welcome me to their humble home and even bring out the family pig to meet me.

The day is hot and muggy and I am anxious to go further up the hill. Leaving the taxi, we walk for about three fourths of a mile in and around bushes, small trees and long grass, until at last I am standing on "Bloody Ridge."

Standing, peering down into the steaming jungle, many visions swirl and cloud my mind. So much so that I don't notice the torrential rain as it beats down soaking my head. With water running off my nose and chin, I walk along the ridge. My clothes become drenched and my shoes soggy, but I am lost in thought. I am looking for the place where I waited and huddled, prayed and slept, those many years ago — My Foxhole.

It is incredible, on this island besieged by war and ravaged by time, that something so fragile as a pit, dug into the earth, could still remain—I feel very humble—it lays before me. Not clean dirt, but with grass growing inside. Climbing down into it, in soggy clothes—they are now muddy, but I don't notice—it is as if no change had ever taken place. I can feel the cold and the misery and looking into the jungle, expecting at any moment for the enemy to begin another charge.

Lying in my home of long ago, my mind visualizes some

of the fierce battles and horrible tricks played upon us by the Japanese soldiers. Two Japanese, wearing only their skivies are walking up the hill, in a token of surrender. Several of our men walked down to meet them and accepted what appeared to be a peace offer. Suddenly the Japenese soldier in front dropped to his knees. There was a machine gun strapped to his back. The other Jap soldier grabbed the trigger, spitting death to the two Marines who had gone to bring them to the "safety" of our lines. I can take no more.

Walking from Bloody Ridge to the taxi, I pick up a shell casing lying on the path. It is from a Japanese 31mm. I wonder what mark the lead from this spent shell had found.

The rain has quit and my clothes are almost dry as we return to the village on the edge of Bloody Ridge. I stand silent as the natives gather beside me for some photos. Taking in everything in sight, I think this must last me a lifetime. I will leave this island forever tomorrow.

Driving back to the hotel, Mendena, in Honiara, I reflect on today. How gullible we were, how trusting of our leaders! True, Franklin Roosevelt was a great leader and gave us much

Native looking into the jungle from "Bloody Ridge," a hiding place for the Japanese soldiers in 1942.

A view of the beach, around the bend from Lunga Point. Much action took place here in 1942.

Author and guide atop "Bloody Ridge," Guadalcanal. The author located his old "foxhole."

support during those times, but the high command, I wonder. I have learned even General Douglas MacArthur didn't believe the Guadalcanal offensive would succeed. And if only Hap Arnold, who was commander of the Army Air Force, had sent us some air support, many Marines would be alive today. I guess it must be true what my father used to say, "Hindsight is always better than foresight."

During the fighting of November 1942, on Guadalcanal, our outfit was kept on the front lines for nearly the entire month. Food was a scarce commodity, thanks in part to the Merchant Marines Union who demanded more money, or they would refuse to bring us the "staff of life." Our menu consisted mainly of C rations. They were old and I understand condemned in the United States. We even enjoyed the hard crackers or "biscuits" that came along with the rations and, believe it or not thought of Spam as a luxury not often available.

Several ships of the United States Navy finally got through to us and sent a field kitchen ashore which was quickly set up behind our lines. Hot food had been just a part of our imagination for some time, so we anxiously awaited our turn to go to dinner. We went in pairs from the line. Not many men could be spared at any one time. It was about three-quarters of a mile and we made the trip on the run. Not only were we anxious for the hot food, but we needed to dodge snipers and "Pistol Pete" (Japanese Artillery) which kept us skipping along, not even chancing an admiring glance at the scenery.

Whenever I watch M-A-S-H I am constantly reminded of the capabilities of following a runner with artillery. I thank God that day no one was hit.

On that run for the rations, Peterson and I arrived at the steaming cookers all laid out among the palm trees. I could almost taste the hot food all the way from the lines. We had been told it would be regular mess, like back at stateside, but we were not prepared for the food which was served.

Eagerly opening the containers, one at a time, we found the first contained boiled onions. The second container, beets. The third was fried cabbage and the succulent meat we had braved death to get to was dozens of boiled tongues. I rubbed my eyes unbelieving, but that is what was served — boiled tongues. They looked like they were just waiting to taste something themselves. I happen to be one of the few men who love cabbage and onions, but as for the tongues, ach!!! I decided to wait for another day to satisfy my taste for meat.

Standing here on Bloody Ridge in 1979, my thoughts return to 1942. December. Almost Christmas. Days are spent cleaning equipment, sleeping — not very much sleep at nights — lots of card playing, talking about home. It seems another time and another world. During those days, two times a week, we had the duty to take a patrol into the steaming jungle, map out the perimeter of the enemy and, at night, stand watch, ever alert to make sure the Japanese soldiers didn't infiltrate our lines.

Nights were a living hell. I am unable to remember a night passing where we didn't engage in some kind of firefight. "Washing Machine Charlie" (a long Japanese plane) flies over almost every night, dropping supplies to their comrades in the jungles, and usually a bomb is dropped on our lines mostly for harrassment. One night a sack of rice was dropped landing on a Jeep causing serious damage to the Jeep. Often a Japanese destroyer or cruiser would slip close to shore and fire broadside into our positions. Our only relief from this harrassment was death or stateside evacuation and you needed to be seriously ill or wounded to be evacuated. Most of the troops had malaria. Malaria brings on a high fever but it is not as serious here as it would be in the States. But, malaria alone didn't qualify you for a stateside ticket.

One Marine who made the stateside journey and one who tried and failed comes to mind. I will call the later one "Jerry." Jerry was a heavily built Jewish boy, not built for walking and hiking comfortably. Many times we could hear him mumbling aloud, "If only I would get just a flesh wound I would be able to go home." None of us ever suspected what was on Jerry's mind.

One morning after spending a hellish night on the line we turned to cleaning our weapons. Jerry carried a B.A.R. (Browning Automatic rifle). He was using his poncho (a sort of rain gear), as shade from the burning sun while cleaning his gear. The morning was shattered by a rifle shot echoing along the ridge, then a cry, "Now I get to go home." There was no way it could be proved but we all felt Jerry had indeed made the self-sacrifice of doing the job himself. Jerry had one problem, the bullet only pierced the fleshy part of his thigh missing a bone. He was given first aid and sent to the field hospital, which was alongside of Henderson field, "A tent city in a field of mud."

About ten days later Jerry was back, unhappy, but resigned to his fate.

The first Marine I remember being sent stateside, not in a box, was a young farmer from Iowa, "Paul." Paul was a fine man and a good Marine, a man to be with when the chips were down. Paul was very inquisitive and collected many souvenirs, even though he knew it would be impossible to take them with us as we moved around. One afternoon Paul picked up a Japanese knee mortar shell. He began throwing rocks at it in an attempt to explode it. Nothing happened. Again he slammed it down, still no explosion. Then, and I can't understand this even today but, he held the shell in his hand, pounded it on a rock, there was a sickening explosion. His hand had received the brunt and it was in shreds. He grabbed his upper arm, the blood was pulsing on the ground. Running to assist him I shall always remember his words that so well reflect the uselessness of war, between cries of pain he said over and over, "God how I wanted to go home, but not this way."

There are many stories which would reflect those early days of fighting on Guadalcanal. Most of them would only strengthen Paul's statement, "The uselessness and the suffering of a war." I was evacuated from Guadalcanal in a converted DC-3 used as a hospital plane. The sides held stretchers and corpsmen walked up and down the aisle during the flight to reassure us. Two other DC-3's left the same time as I for New Zealand. We were informed the pilot was flying close to the water as the Japanese Zero's were not able to maneuver at that low altitude.

Upon arriving at the hospital in New Zealand, we learned the other two planes were missing.

The hospital was staffed with U.S. Navy nurses, very spit and polished from what I had been used to. My socks hadn't been changed for three weeks and upon arrival and removing my shoes I found I had no bottoms, just tops. I get a nostalgic feeling when I see Red Skelton in a skit of "Freddie the Freeloader," as that is the way we must have looked.

At the New Zealand Hospital an incident occurred I shall always remember. A young Navy Lieutenant, nurse, trying to be spit and polish G.I., came into our quarters which contained about twenty-five patients, and said, "There will be an inspection in one hour; all patients who can get out of bed will be beside their cots, standing or sitting, with their drawers open." When she realized what she had said, with a blush and a smart about-face she said, "Carry on," and left the room. We had no inspection that day.

Another incident I shall always treasure: Bill Miller (not his true name), had been shot in the private sector and was a pitiful sight to behold. He was very despondent and had tears in his eyes on many occasions as he talked of the new bride he had left behind and the family he now felt he could never have. Then one morning he awoke and, with a yell you could hear in Wellington, brought the rest of us to life. With his hand around his member, which was sticking straight out, he yelled, "It works! It works!" The nurse came running to see what was the matter. He still had it cradled in his hand and proudly proclaimed to her, "It works! It works!" Without a sound, the nurse left but was back in a few minutes with a small bottle of brandy that comes in the medical kits and, handing it to Miller, said, "You certainly deserve to have a celebration." There was only about two shots in those bottles, but each one of us toasted to his good luck.

As the Air Pacific taxies from the small airport up the airstrip and turns for its final leg of the journey before taking off from Henderson Field, I can see clearly the tower, Bloody Ridge, lying in a mist of clouds. And many other landmarks I remembered from 1943. However, it is not the same. I am sitting in the first class section looking out the window this time. In 1943 I was flat on my back in the stretcher fastened to the cabin walls of the converted DC-3 unable to see anything outside the airplane on the evacuation to New Zealand.

I was on my way to a recovery area to receive treatment for malaria, yellow jaundice and dysentery that had made me so weak I could hardly raise my head. Malaria, alone, was a way of life and did not qualify you for the trip. Just a little rest, a few quinine pills and back to the action of patrols. Yellow jaundice was another disease not too prominent in the U.S.A. We all took adibrane tablets which was a substitute for quinine and the yellow dye did make most of us a little yellow in color but the disease jaundice made a man of a different color so to speak. Your eyes would get yellow, your spleen enlarged and hurt and it was impossible to keep anything down. If you did manage to get something down, the dysentery took care of that. What a miserable combination of problems!

I lay on Bloody Ridge for about a week with malaria and then yellow jaundice before I was sent back to the hospital at

Henderson Field. During that week the corpsmen assigned to our platoon gave me a can of condensed milk every other day. That is all I was supposed to take internally for my illness.

It is remarkable, the life we lived. When we hurt and are miserable, we almost pray for God to take us and end this miserable torture but, as the planes bombed the hospital tents each day and the Japanese brought a gunboat close to the beach one night, firing point blank, and with the incessant whistling of Washing Machine Charlie's lone bomb every evening, we gathered ourselves up and, although swore it was impossible to move, managed to dive into foxholes or shellholes each time danger threatened. Just to preserve the life you felt was so miserable.

Then up the coast of Guadalcanal and out over the ocean, I would sleep and dream of those days gone by. My next main stop would be the return to New Zealand. I wondered aloud if I would remember anyone or anything. Would it be changed so much? I would soon know.

CHAPTER XII

LAND OF THE MUTTONBURGERS

It is New Years Day 1980 and I am in Auckland, New Zealand. It had been thirty-seven years since my last visit. My mind is jumping at the thought of steak and eggs, along with huge pitchers of cold milk, which I enjoyed so much in those days of 1943.

After checking in at the hotel, I decided to look around a little, and stopping in one of the many small shops around the waterfront, I look for some articles I will need for shaving. The lady who waits on me is grey-haired and looks quite old and mentions, "You aren't from here, are you?" I said no, I wasn't. "Where do you come from?" When I told her I had been there thirty-seven years ago as a young Marine, she told me a story of her sneaking out at night to meet with some of the Marines and go to the dances. She said, "You Yanks were a lot of fun, and rich, too. Our parents didn't want us to go with the likes of you as they thought you were all over-sexed."

She added, "I was just seventeen in those days." I gulped, took a second look, quickly glanced in the mirror and looked back at her. Up to that time I had thought of looking up some of the girls I had dated, but when I looked again, I decided I would let well enough alone. For the first time on my journey, I felt finally old.

It was time to look over the country. I rented a car and drove the narrow highways and byways on the wrong side of the road to Wellington and then up to Paekakariki where our camp had been. My memory was of our tent city stretching out for miles, a mass of tents, and across the tracks at McCays Crossing the 6th Regiment. I remembered it as a huge area but now, thirty-seven years later, it looked no bigger than a small farm. The hills were still there where we hiked and climbed. The tavern was still standing, but everything looked so small; it looked like it was in miniature. It just wasn't the same.

New Zealand holds many fond memories. It is like an oasis after Guadalcanal — an island of bread and honey. In 1943 my first meeting with New Zealanders came several weeks after I had been transferred from the main hospital to the two-man huts next to the hospital at Auckland. We were allowed to come and go as we pleased as long as we checked in regularly. I really never felt up to it as the malaria kept recurring and it is an energy-sapping ordeal. We would wander around the grounds and look up at the civilian hospital.

I remember one afternoon. It was a particularly warm and summery day. Several of us were eyeing a group of young ladies who were flirting back at us from the second floor of the hospital and motioning for us to come up and join them. We all decided to go in a group. After all there were enough to go around. Upon entering the front door, we were stopped by the nurse in charge who asked us what we were doing there. We told her of our experience in flirting with the girls on the second floor and felt it was an invitation for us to up. Imagine our chagrin when we were told that the section where the lovely ladies were waving from was the V.D. section of the hospital. I needn't add we went meekly back to our own quarters.

Ah, yes, those were the days. We were treated like kings.

Field in Paekakariki where the mighty Second was bivouacked.

196

McCays Crossing, New Zealand, just above Paekakariki. The Second Regiment was at this location for nine months.

That is, for most of the time while in New Zealand. It wasn't until I returned some thirty-eight years later I discovered the main reason behind it. We were not aware, but just a few days before the mighty 2nd Marine Division arrived in Wellington Bay from Guadalcanal, there had been numerous sightings of Japanese submarines within Wellington Harbor. Many New Zealanders were selling their holdings as fast as they could find any buyer and prices were cheap. The New Zealand population felt sure that a Japanese invasion was on the way.

Of course we had some bloody battles right in downtown Wellington but not with any Japanese. Whenever any English ship would arrive or a New Zealand soldier would come home on leave and find his girl with an American, the fight would start.

My memory belies with the thought of the two New Zealanders who had a special love for the United States Marines in so many ways. A father and son, "Charlie Brazier," a fiddler and his son "Ron," who though small in stature (a dwarf), he was huge in heart and in his dedicated worship of the

Marines. Charlie, too old for the service, would finish his day job then clean up, and strapping his fiddle to the frame of his bicycle pedal the 10 miles to town so he could play his special kind of music for free at the old Cecil Club, which was turned into the U.S.O. He also played at the Grant and Wakefield Hotel for special dances. Ron Brazier, his son, was much more than a "Marine mascot." He shared a special kind of love for his adopted family of the 2nd Marine Division.

On my return to New Zealand Ron proudly displayed hundreds of pictures and stacks of letters from his adoptive families, nothing was ever thrown away if it was connected in any way to "his Marines."

It was a real love affair between the New Zealanders and Marines which exists to this day.

Our camp at Paekakariki was a former sheep ranch and was right in among a lot of hills and ridges. This gave us the exercise we needed to sweat out the beer and those long hikes and forced marches were kind of fun. We also enjoyed many goods times as occur in most camps if one but looks on the good side. One party I remember: a beer party with lots of stout which was strong beer and came in quarts, large quarts, and we all drank our share. At the party was Dr. Green, a Navy doctor. All doctors assigned to the Marines were Navy; we had none

Over the hill from McCays crossing to Paekakariki.

of our own. We lovingly called him "Greeno the Marino." All officers were supposed to be spit and polish when not on the lines. They said it bred discipline. Well, during the course of the evening, I went into the head (toilet) to relieve myself. I was standing at the urinal when Lt. Green (Greeno-the-Marino) came in to relieve himself. As we both stood at the urinal relieving ourselves, I noticed a stream going astray so I warned Dr. Green to that effect (he stood a good chance of getting drenched). Dr. Green looked at me through bloodshot eyes and said, in a slurring but commanding voice, "That's all root, Twitch. You piss on me and I'll piss on you and nobody will be mad at nobody."

We all looked forward to the First Lady visiting us — "Eleanor Roosevelt" — and after she left, some punchinello left a sign on the outhouse that said, "Eleanor sat here."

The land of New Zealand, according to the history and stories passed down by the inhabitants, with all it's hills and ridges, was a hunk of land too large for the place in the ocean, it was to be. So God gathered it up in his hands, bunched it together making the topography as it is today.

A lot of the time on New Zealand, during the war years, was spent listening to Tokyo Rose. We never did find out where

she got her scoop which she kept broadcasting. Even after the war, I never found out.

There were many widows and fatherless children left in New Zealand after the battle of Tarawa and even more after the Saipan landing. One of these fatherless I met on my return home. He was an airline steward on Air New Zealand. His jump seat was right in front of me so I had occasion to speak to him often on that long flight from New Zealand to Los Angeles. His name was Clark. He told me his mother had married a Marine of the 2nd Division and he was born several months after the Battle of Tarawa. Although Clark had never met his father he told me he sees him in all the Marines that come aboard his flight. I was able to detect a feeling of proudness in his voice, as misty-eyed, he told me of his mother's faith and the love she shared with her Marine husband and his Marine father.

The only battlefield which I didn't return to was Saipan in the Marianas. Maybe another time. Saipan was a hard-fought war within itself. Even though I was an active participant in the assault until D plus 5 when gunshot wounds forced my evacuation to Guadalcanal for hospitalization, I was soon returned to full duty at Saipan which consisted of many patrols made to clear specific areas of the remaining enemy. I still don't feel qualified to write the story of the entire battle that occur-

Wellington, New Zealand.

red there. I have however, throughout my book, told of incidents that occurred on Saipan as well as other beachheads of which I have personal knowledge.

Upon returning home from the 22,000 mile journey into the past, I often catch myself returning to those islands in thoughts and dreams, but they are now pleasant thoughts and peaceful dreams. The exorcism has been a complete success.

"LEST WE FORGET." Military services on Betio, Tarawa for those felled in battle November 20, 1943.

CHAPTER XIII

"LEST WE FORGET"

Although a great effort was made by myself, I found it was not possible to transcribe into words that which I felt could or would convey to the reader my true feelings upon returning to the Tarawa atolls, after an absence of over thirty-eight years.

It was especially difficult for me, upon the discovery and surfacing from "out of its tomb" a well-preserved amphibious tractor, "alligator," and from inside this machine of war finding the remains of three United States Marines. These Marines were killed in that holocaust, "Tarawa." One of the remains still carried the dog tags of Arthur D. Somes. The name "Arthur D. Somes" marks the grave of another buried in Arlington National Cemetery, according to records of the United States Navy.

I have labeled what happened during the two and one-half years following the discovery of the amphibious tank as an "Act of Callousness" by some of our government officials and their seeming indifference when requested to right that wrong, an error committed thirty-five years ago. At that time it probably was an honest mistake, but a mistake that could be corrected now with but just a few strokes of a pen.

In writing this chapter, I wish to make known my heartfelt gratitude and warm thanks to my friend, and United States Senator, the Honorable Henry M. Jackson. Senator Jackson, or "Scoop" to his friends, listened, wrote letters and was instrumental in finally returning the remains of my buddies and "America's heroes" home. Home to rest at last in the land they fought to preserve.

That the reader may know the frustrations I suffered in my drive to accomplish this tremendous task, the next twenty-six pages contain letters between government officials and myself. I would hope, after reading them, you will have a better insight into the workings of our government, as well as the thinking of those in charge.

I make no comment on the letters or their content; they speak for themselves. I only ask your understanding.

Marine's body found on atoll

The Seattle Times **Monday, February 11, 1980**
by Don Duncan
Times staff reporter

This nation's highly publicized efforts to recover the remains of Americans killed in Vietnam apparently do not extend to the now-distant World War II.

So, to the parents of Pfc. Arthur D. Somes, killed in action November 23, 1943, on Betio, Tarawa Atoll:

Your son's body finally has been found.

The body you had buried in Arlington Cemetery November 7, 1947, is another "unknown soldier."

Somes and two of his fellow marines were in an amphibian tractor when

---

" . . . the Japanese still come to the atoll to find their ancestors; are we so uncivilized and nonfeeling that we forget those who gave their lives for us?"

---

it was buried in the sand.

All three were in full battle dress in the well-preserved amtrack, unearthed in October during a sewer-digging project outside a native hut.

Somes still had his dog tags around his neck. The others did not.

Robert R. Twitchell of Everett, on a nostaglic visit to the places where he fought as a marine during World War II, came across the "amtrack" in December.

Twitchell viewed the remains of the three marines taken from the vehicle. He was told that the bones of others had been found on the island.

Officials of the Ministry of Betio told Twitchell they contacted the Nimitz Foundation in Texas concerning the discovery of the "amtrack' and its three bodies.

The foundation, in turn, contacted appropriate officials in Washington, D.C.

The native government told Twitchell it was informed, in effect, "we no longer are interested."

"Appalled at the callousness of some officials of the United States government," Twitchell, a former Snohomish County sheriff, fired off a letter to Senator Henry Jackson.

In the letter, Twitchell noted that "the Japanese still come to the atoll to find their ancestors; are we so uncivilized and nonfeeling that we forget those who gave their lives for us?"

Jackson quickly responded that he had contacted the Marine Corps and would await a reply.

That reply has come.

Weapons, rusted in shallow water or half buried in the sand, and Japanese pillboxes, scarred by mortar fire, are mute testimony of the 4,500 Japanese and 1,500 Americans who died during the fighting.

Pfc. Arthur D. Somes had been killed in action on Betio, Tarawa Atoll, November 20, 1943. His remains had been moved to Arlington National Cemetery, Washington, D.C., November 7, 1947, "at his mother's request."

Meanwhile, the natives of Tarawa carefully are preserving the "real" remains of Somes and his companions.

They have learned to live with the relics of war, said Twitchell, who was with the first waves of the 2nd Marine Division to hit the Betio beach in November, 1943.

Weapons, rusted in shallow water or half buried in the sand, and Japanese pillboxes, scarred by mortar fire, are mute testimony to the 4,500 Japanese and 1,500 Americans who died during the bloody fighting there.

So pleased were the natives to see Corporal Twitchell — "the first American war veteran to come to Betio in eight years" — that they hailed him as a great returning war hero.

Messages were flashed by radio the length of the atoll.

Twitchell also visited Guadalcanal, where his marine company landed before Tarawa.

There he sought out Sgt. Maj. Jacob Vousa, the highly publicized native who survived a Japanese bayoneting to set up a network of scouts to guide Americans throughout the Solomon Islands campaign.

A 20-mile jeep ride back into the hills produced the now white-haired Vousa, an American flag flying from a flagpole next to a large stone monument and plaque erected by the British government after Vousa was knighted for his work by the Queen.

"It was some thrill to find our flag flying out there in the jungle," Twitchell said.

In another village, perhaps 40 miles distant, Twitchell found a jungle clearing filled with the battered remains of warplanes that didn't survive the battle of Guadalcanal. A native tends it as a sort of shrine.

"Everywhere you look over there are reminders of the battles fought over 36 years ago," Twitchell said. "I even found my old foxhole on the side of a grassy hill.

"We tend to forget back home."

As for Pfc. Arthur Somes' body, Twitchell said:

"I always knew it had to be, of course. But now I have proof that there is more than one 'Unknown Soldier' in Arlington Cemetery."

United States Senate

COMMITTEE ON ARMED SERVICES

WASHINGTON, D.C. 20510

January 8, 1980

Mr. Robert R. Twitchell
5719 Cady Road
Everett, Washington 98203

Dear Bob:

Thank you for your letter written on Christmas Day in the Solomon Islands. I am sure it was quite a change for you from your last "visit" there in 1943.

I was sorry to have your report, and in an effort to obtain an explanation have contacted the Marine Corps in this regard.

When I hear from them, I will write to you again.

With all good wishes,

Sincerely yours,

Henry M. Jackson, U.S.S.

HMJ:kl

JOHN C. STENNIS, MISS., CHAIRMAN

HENRY M. JACKSON, WASH.   JOHN TOWER, TEX.
HOWARD W. CANNON, NEV.   STROM THURMOND, S.C.
HARRY F. BYRD, JR., VA.   BARRY GOLDWATER, ARIZ.
SAM NUNN, GA.   JOHN W. WARNER, VA.
JOHN C. CULVER, IOWA   GORDON J. HUMPHREY N.H.
GARY HART, COLO.   WILLIAM S. COHEN, MAINE
ROBERT MORGAN, N.C.   ROGER W. JEPSEN, IOWA
J. JAMES EXON, NEBR.
CARL LEVIN, MICH.

FRANCIS J. SULLIVAN, STAFF DIRECTOR

United States Senate

COMMITTEE ON ARMED SERVICES
WASHINGTON, D.C. 20510

January 24, 1980

Mr. Robert R. Twitchell
5719 Cady Road
Everett, Washington 98203

Dear Bob:

In further reference to our exchange
of correspondence, I am enclosing a copy of
the letter I have just received from the
Marine Corps in answer to my inquiry concerning the finding of remains of personnel
in Tarawa, Karabiti.

It is hard to understand that one of
the Marines had Arthur D. Somes' tags in view
of the statement contained in the enclosed
letter.

I am glad to know that letters were
sent from Headquarters, Marine Corps concerning
Mr. Falkland's discoveries. Since he has not
responded, it is possible that the letters went
astray. At least they are still interested in
accounting for the remains of the Marines who
were lost during the campaign.

Best regards.

Sincerely yours,

Henry M. Jackson, U.S.S.

HMJ:kt
Encl.

209

Department of the Navy
Headquarters United States Marine Corps
Washington, D.C. 20380

MSPA-1/mvp
3040
22 JAN 1980

The Honorable Henry M. Jackson
United States Senate
Washington, D.C. 20510

Dear Senator Jackson:

This is in response to your letter of January 8, 1980, concerning remains recently found in Tarawa, Karabiti (formerly Gilbert Islands).

This Headquarters is aware of the fact that remains of personnel have been discovered by Mr. Falkland. Two letters were sent from this Headquarters on October 1, 1979, and December 12, 1979, to Mr. Falkland, requesting his assistance concerning knowledge of the location of the remains of U.S. Marine Corps casualties from World War II. Mr. Falkland has not responded to either of these letters.

In regard to Private First Class Arthur D. SOMES, U.S. Marine Corps, the records available at this Headquarters have been researched and indicate that Private First Class Somes was killed in action at Tarawa, Gilbert Island on November 20, 1943, and his remains were reinterred in grave #2784, Section #12, Arlington National Cemetery, Fort Myer, Virginia on November 7, 1947 at his mother's request.

Because no accounting has been made for the remains of many of our Marines lost during the Tarawa campaign, any conjecture as to the actual identity of the recently recovered remains would be premature. Accordingly, this matter has been referred to the Decedent Affairs Branch of the Bureau of Medicine and Surgery, Department of the Navy, Washington, D.C. 20372 for assistance.

Your interest in Marine Corps matters is appreciated and I trust the foregoing information satisfactorily answers your letter.

Sincerely,

ROY L. BELLI
Colonel, U.S. Marine Corps
Director, Personnel Services Division
By direction of the
Commandant of the Marine Corps

10 February 1980

Col. Roy L. Belli
U.S. Marine Corps.
Washington, D.C. 20380

Dear Colonel:

I am in receipt of a copy of your letter of January 22, 1980 to Senator Henry
M. Jackson in response to his letter of January 8th, 1980 concerning remains
recently found on Betio (Tarawa Atoll,) Karabiti, Formerly Gilbert Islands.

The third paragraph of your letter intrigues me and the fourth paragraph
baffles me.

I am fully aware that a person sitting at a desk must field questions in
such a manner as to confuse and also to keep the questioner from asking
further questions -- but I was there -- then on November 20 - 23, 1943
and now December 14 - 21st, 1979.

Many of my buddies were killed by the Japanese on that Atoll, (Betio) and
I would not like to believe their memories could be erased so easily.

They have a right and you have a duty -- possibly not a legal right or duty
but a moral one -- to be buried under their christan name on American soil
if they can be identified. Isn"t that what dog tags are for?

I would ask -- no demand -- you take affirmative action to correct any
wrongs that can be corrected in properly identifying our dead heroes.

> Once a Marine
> always a Marine

CC: Senator Henry M. Jackson

Bob Twitchell
U.S. M. C 432368
5719 Cady Rd.
Everett
Washington 98203

211

The Honorable Henry M. Jackson
United States Senate
Washington, D. C. 20510

Dear Senator Jackson:

The Commandant, United States Marine Corps, forwarded
your letter of 8 January 1980 to this Bureau for response concerning recovery of remains at Betio, Tarawa.

This Bureau has general staff responsibility for care and
disposition of deceased naval personnel. The Department of the
Army was assigned responsibility for accountability and repatriation of remains of Armed Services Personnel following World War
II. Accordingly, an inquiry was made to the Commander, Casualty
and Memorial Affairs, Department of the Army, for review of their
records concerning "Arthur D. Somes". Their records are in
consonance with records the Marine Corps Casualty Section maintain indicating that Private First Class Somes was interred at
Arlington National Cemetery on 7 November 1947.

The Army Central Identification Laboratory, Hawaii (CIL-HI)
will initiate an inquiry to Government Officials at Tarawa. When
it can be verified through official sources that the remains may
be United States Marine Corps personnel, arrangements will be made
for a visit to Betio, Tarawa by CIL-HI personnel for personal
inspection of the remains.

Several trips by Army Graves Registration (GR) personnel from
Hawaii have been made previously based on information received
similar to your constituent's report. In those instances, the
remains were identified as Japanese. Statements, alleging a lack
of interest in remains, may have been made after determining they
were Japanese.

You may be assured that the Department of the Army will make
a thorough investigation into the report of recovered Marine Corps
remains. In the event they are individually identified as Marine

Corps personnel, arrangements will be made to return them to their
next of kin in keeping with procedures governing this very sensitive function.

Your interest in this matter is appreciated.

Sincerely,

W. P. ARENTZEN
Vice Admiral, Medical Corps

212

JOHN C. STENNIS, MISS., CHAIRMAN

HENRY M. JACKSON, WASH.   JOHN TOWER, TEX.
HOWARD W. CANNON, NEV.   STROM THURMOND, S.C.
HARRY F. BYRD, JR., VA.   BARRY GOLDWATER, ARIZ.
SAM NUNN, GA.   JOHN W. WARNER, VA.
JOHN C. CULVER, IOWA   GORDON J. HUMPHREY N.H.
GARY HART, COLO.   WILLIAM S. COHEN, MAINE
ROBERT MORGAN, N.C.   ROGER W. JEPSEN, IOWA
J. JAMES EXON, NEBR.
CARL LEVIN, MICH.

FRANCIS J. SULLIVAN, STAFF DIRECTOR

𝕌nited 𝕊tates 𝕊enate

COMMITTEE ON ARMED SERVICES
WASHINGTON, D.C. 20510

February 27, 1980

Mr. Robert R. Twitchell
5719 Cady Road
Everett, Washington 98203

Dear Bob:

Since writing to you on January 24,
I have received further information from
the Department of the Navy in answer to my
inquiry concerning the remains recently
found in Tarawa.

I am enclosing a copy of the second
letter I have received, which would indicate
that steps have been and are being taken to
check into this serious matter.

I have been informally advised that it
is entirely possible that PFC Somes' dog tags
could have been separated from his body.

I have seen the article in the Seattle
Times regarding your visit.

Best wishes.

Sincerely yours,

Henry M. Jackson, U.S.S.

HMJ:kt
Encl.

213

March 3, 1980

Vice Admiral W.P. Arntzen
United States Navy
WashingtonD.C. 20380

Dear Sir:

I am in receipt of several letters from the United States
Marine Corps and the United States Navy, (I enclose copies along with
my original letter to Senator Jackson.) It would appear to me someone
is more interested in covering up a bad situation than in finding out
the facts and giving our dead heroes a proper burial and recognition.

Some of the facts are, I was there, Betio, "Tarawa" on November 20th 1943 in the first assault wave with the 2 - 2 - 2 G. Co.
3rd. Platoon, and again on a nostalgic visit December 14-15-16-17 of
1979. I talked with the natives, I talked with the government officials
on the Atoll, I saw the evidence, I am convinced. I also took many
pictures and discussed the posibility of a mix up, but the evidence as
I viewed and studied it convinces me someone in Washington D.C. used
bad judgement and no one on Tarawa is to blame. I consider myself a
capable investigator having served as Chief of Police and twice elected
County Sheriff.'

I would ask, in view of the circumstances, I be included on
any trip to Betio, "Tarawa," to see this deplorable situation brought
to its proper conclusion.

Respectfully

Robert R. "Bob"Twitchell
U.S.M.C. 423268
5719 Cady Rd.
Everett, Wa 98203

C.C. Commandant
U.S.M.S.
Washington D.C.

Senator Henry M. Jackson
Washington, D.C.

IN REPLY REFER TO
MS:gjb
12 MAR 1980

Mr. Bob Twitchell
5719 Cady Road
Everett, Washington 98203

Dear Sir:

Your letter dated February 10, 1980, and post marked
March 3, 1980, has just been received.

This Headquarters was aware of the remains which had been
discovered on Tarawa and had made two unsuccessful attempts
to contact Mr. Falkland for assistance prior to your
bringing the matter to our attention through Senator Jackson.
The matter was referred to the Chief, Bureau of Medicine
and Surgery (BUMED), who has general staff responsibility for
the care and disposition of deceased naval personnel. Since
the Department of the Army was assigned responsibility for
accountability and repatriation of remains of armed services
personnel following World War II, BUMED queried the Commander,
Casualty and Memorial Affairs, Department of the Army for a
review of records concerning Private First Class Somes. Those
records are in consonance with the records of this Headquarters
indicating Private First Class Somes was interred at Arlington
National Cemetery on November 7, 1947. Nevertheless, the
Army Central Identification Laboratory in Hawaii is scheduled
to send a recovery team to Tarawa this month to inspect the
remains which have been discovered.

There has been no attempt to delay or confuse. I am quite
aware of my duty. In all cases involving deceased Marines
our primary concern is for the next of kin. When a thorough
investigation is completed by the Department of the Army, and,
if the remains are identified as Marine Corps personnel,
arrangements will be made to return them to their next of kin
in keeping with procedures governing this very sensitive function.
Until such time, it would be heartless to resurrect and com-
pound the grief which may have been eased by the passage of
over three decades.

Sincerely,

ROY L. BELLI
Colonel, U. S. Marine Corps
Director, Personnel Services Division
By direction of the Commandant of the Marine Corps

Copy to: Senator Jackson

DEPARTMENT OF THE NAVY
BUREAU OF MEDICINE AND SURGERY
WASHINGTON, D.C. 20372

IN REPLY REFER TO
MED:3134:AFE:rgk
Ser: 00310050
24 March 1980

Mr. Robert R. "Bob" Twitchell
U.S.M.C. 423268
5719 Cady Road
Everett, Washington 98203

Dear Mr. Twitchell:

This is in response to your letter of March 3, 1980 concerning the
remains of Marine Corps personnel at Tarawa.

This Bureau is without the authority to investigate the circumstances and examine remains recovered at Betio. The Department
of the Army was assigned such authority by Congress and is
responsible for resolution of World War II deceased military
personnel.

We are informed that personnel assigned at the Central Identification Laboratory, Hawaii (CIL-HI), who are trained in Graves
Registration (GR) procedures and specialists in human remains
identification, will depart Hawaii for Tarawa at the end of
March. Their primary mission is to conduct an investigation
concerning the circumstances and to examine the remains recovered
at Betio.

In view of the information indicated above your request for
approval to be included in travel to Tarawa with the CIL-HI team
should appropriately be submitted to the Army.

It is regretted that a more favorable report cannot be provided.
If this Bureau can be of further assistance, please do not
hesitate to contact us.

Sincerely,

H. H. SOWERS, JR.
CAPT, MSC, USN
Director, Health Benefits Division
By direction of the Surgeon General

Robert R. "Bob" Twitchell
5719 Cady Road
Everett, Washington 98203

H.H. Sowers Jr., Capt. MSC USN
Director, Health Benefits Division
Department of the Navy
Bureau of Medicine and Surgery
Washington D.C. 20372

RE: 3134: AFE: rgk (letter enc.)
Ser: 00310050

June 14, 1980

Dear Captain Sowers:

Three months have passed since my last communication from you regarding the remains recovered on Betio. I would hope your investigation has been completed and your office has a copy of the findings. I am requesting a copy of this report so I may know my comrades and buddies were given the recognition they deserve and can assure my many friends of the responsiveness of our government.

Many thanks to you and those who worked to bring this sensitive case to its conclusion.

Sincerely,

Robert R. "Bob" Twitchell
U.S.M.C. 432368 Hon. Disch.

CC: Senator Jackson

DEPARTMENT OF THE NAVY
BUREAU OF MEDICINE AND SURGERY
WASHINGTON, D.C. 20372

IN REPLY REFER TO
MED:3134:AFE:ace
26 June 1980

Mr. Robert R. "Bob" Twitchell
5719 Cady Road
Everett, Washington 98203

Dear Mr. Twitchell:

This is in response to your letter of 14 June 1980 concerning the remains of
Marine Corps personnel at Tarawa.

I am informed unofficially that remains were recovered at Betio and are currently
under identification processing at the Army's Central Identification Laboratory,
Hawaii (CIL-HI). A request has been received for health and dental records
for two Marine Corps members for comparison with the physical characteristics
of the recovered remains.

It would be indiscreet and presumptuous to provide names of those believed to
be involved pending complete examination of the remains and records by the
Forensic Anthropologist. It is hoped you may understand and appreciate my
position and the sensitivity of the situation.

When Army's (CIL-HI) personnel have concluded their evaluations, I will be
advised officially of the identification findings/recommendations and will be
at liberty to divulge such information subsequent to appropriate notification
of family members.

Your interest in this matter is appreciated. If this Bureau can be of further
assistance, please do not hesitate to contact us.

Sincerely,

H. H. SOWERS, JR.
CAPT, MSC, USN
Director, Health Benefits Division
By direction of the Surgeon General

Robert R Bob Twitchell
5719 Cady Road
Everett, Washington
98203

Ref: Med: 3134 AFE :rgk
July 4th 1980

Department of the Navy
Bureau of Medicine and Surgery
Washington, D.C. 2037

ATTN: Captain H.H. Sowers Jr. MSC USN

Dear Captain Sowers:

Thank you for your letter of June 24th 1980. I am most
relieved that at long last my forgotten buddies will be put to rest
under their rightful identification.

I would make one more request, that upon identification by
the Army's Centeral Identification Laboratory, Hawaii, (CIL HI) and
proper nXtification of next of kin I be given the names of those forgotten heroes, so that my mind may also be put to rest.

Thanks again for your help, interest and cooperation.

Sincerely

Robert R. "Bob" Twitchell

CC SENATOR HENRY M. JACKSON

219

Robert R. Bob Twitchell
5719 Cady Rd.
Everett, Wa 98203

The Honorable Henry M. Jackson
United States Senate
Washington D.C. 21510

                    January 20th 1981

          RE: Enclosed copies of letters:

#1.   Dated March 12th 1980 From Dept of Navy
#2.   Dated March 24th 1980 From Dept of Navy
#3.   Dated June 14th 1980 To the Dept of Navy
#4.   Dated June 26th 1980 From Dept of Navy
#5.   Dated July   4th 1980 To the Dept of Navy

Dear Scoop:

          Since over six months have passed since my last communication from
the Department of the Navy on this sensative matter I am again appealing to
to you for assistance.

          I would be most appreciative if you could help me in my quest.
Thanks again for all your help in the past and I look forward to seeing
you when I come to Washington D.C. which I pplan in the fall.

                              Truly yours

                              Robert R. Bob Twitchell

United States Senate

COMMITTEE ON ARMED SERVICES
WASHINGTON, D.C. 20510

January 26, 1981

Mr. Robert R. Twitchell
5719 Cady Road
Everett, Washington 98203

Dear Bob:

Thank you for your note of January 20 in further reference to identification of the remains that were discovered on Tarawa.

In an effort to obtain an updated report, I have contacted the appropriate officials of the Department of the Navy again in this regard.

When I receive a response from them, I will write to you again.

With best wishes.

Sincerely yours,

Henry M. Jackson, U.S.S.

HMJ:zdb

221

JOHN C. STENNIS, MISS., CHAIRMAN

HENRY M. JACKSON, WASH.   JOHN TOWER, TEX.
HOWARD W. CANNON, NEV.   STROM THURMOND, S.C.
HARRY F. BYRD, JR., VA.   BARRY GOLDWATER, ARIZ.
SAM NUNN, GA.   JOHN W. WARNER, VA.
JOHN C. CULVER, IOWA   GORDON J. HUMPHREY N.H.
GARY HART, COLO.   WILLIAM S. COHEN, MAINE
ROBERT MORGAN, N.C.   ROGER W. JEPSEN, IOWA
'AMES EXON, NEBR.
. LEVIN, MICH.

FRANCIS J. SULLIVAN, STAFF DIRECTOR

United States Senate

COMMITTEE ON ARMED SERVICES

WASHINGTON, D.C. 20510

February 25, 1981

Mr. Robert R. Twitchell
5719 Cady Road
Everett, Washington 98203

Dear Bob:

In further reference to our previous correspondence, I am enclosing a copy of the letter I
received from the Department of the Navy in answer
to my inquiry in your behalf. I believe it is
self-explanatory.

Inasmuch as the Naval Bureau of Medicine and
Surgery was unable to predict a timetable for final
determination, I will conduct a follow-up of this
matter with the Casualty and Memorial Affairs
Division.

When I have received a response from them,
I will get back in touch with you.

Best regards.

Sincerely yours,

Scoop

Henry M. Jackson, U.S.S.

HMJ:zdb

Enclosure

222

DEPARTMENT OF THE NAVY
BUREAU OF MEDICINE AND SURGERY
WASHINGTON, D.C. 20372

FEB 24 12 05 AM '81

IN REPLY REFER TO
MED:3134:AFE:ace
20 February 1981

The Honorable Henry M. Jackson
United States Senate
Washington, D. C. 20510

Dear Senator Jackson:

This is in response to your letter of 26 January 1981 to Headquarters, Marine
Corps concerning the identification of remains recovered at Betio, Tarawa.

The Director, Casualty and Memorial Affairs Division, Department of the Army
has informed authorities at this Bureau that identification processing of
remains has been accomplished by personnel assigned to the Central Identification Laboratory, Hawaii (CIL-HI). Seventeen remains were identified as
Japanese and arrangements are being made to return them to Japan. Two remains
were identified as Marine Corps members and documentation was forwarded by the
Central Identification Laboratory, Hawaii recommending acceptance of identification.

After a review, the Director, Casualty and Memorial Affairs Division, Department
of the Army, as chairman of the Armed Services Graves Registration Office (ASGRO),
will convene a meeting of representatives of the Armed Services. The alternatives
are acceptance, rejection or a recommendation for further evaluation of remains
by the Central Identification Laboratory, Hawaii. In view of the information
indicated, I am unable to provide a timetable for the subsequent functions of
personal notification and the return of remains.

This Bureau in conjunction with the Commandant, Marine Corps is responsible for
the naval current death program functions; however, matters of this nature are
under the control of the Armed Services Graves Registration Office. Future
correspondence concerning this subject should be forwarded directly to the
Director, Casualty and Memorial Affairs Division (DAAG-PED), 2461 Eisenhower
Avenue, Room 984, Alexandria, Virginia 22331.

Your interest in this matter is appreciated.

Sincerely,

H. H. SOWERS, JR.
CAPT, MSC, USN
Director, Health Benefits Division
By direction of the Surgeon General

223

DEPARTMENT OF THE ARMY
Office of the Adjutant General
Washington, D.C. 20310

DAAG - PED

Honorable Henry M. Jackson
United States Senate
Washington, D.C. 20510

Dear Senator Jackson:

This is in response to your letter of 25 February 1981 on behalf of Mr. Robert Twitchell concerning the identification of remains recoverd at Betio, Tarawa.

Documentation concerning identification of remains recovered at Betio, Tarawa has been received from the Central Identification Laboratory, Hawaii. The case files are being reviewed and assembled for Board action. Anticipate final recommendation within 30 days.

Sincerely,

WILLIAM R. FLICK
LTC, GS
Chief, Memorial Affairs Division

Dear Mr. Twitchell:

When I receive information regarding final recommendation, I will forward it to you.

Henry M. Jackson, U.S.S.

Robert R. Bob Twitchell
5719 Cady Road
Everett, Washington 98203

The Honorable Henry M. Jackson
United States Senate
Washington D.C. 21510

July 15th 1981

Dear Scoop:

Many thanks for all you have done in helping me resolve the
disposition of the three (3) United States Marines whose remains were
found on Tarrawa and returned for identification, as per letter dated
Feb. 20th 1981 from the Surgeon General, a copy of which is enclosed
along with a copy of your last letter of transmittel.

I would request any follow up furnished from the Surgeon General
as to evaluation and disposition of the remains of the United States Marines.

Thanks again for your help and best wishes to you on Capital Hill
as it looks like a long hot summer, I am glad you always manage to remain
cool.

Sincerely

Robert R. Bob Twitchell

HENRY M. JACKSON
WASHINGTON

ROOM 137
RUSSELL SENATE OFFICE BUILDING
WASHINGTON, D.C. 20510
(202) 224-3441

𝔘𝔫𝔦𝔱𝔢𝔡 𝔖𝔱𝔞𝔱𝔢𝔰 𝔖𝔢𝔫𝔞𝔱𝔢
WASHINGTON, D.C.

COMMITTEES:
ENERGY AND
NATURAL RESOURCES
ARMED SERVICES
GOVERNMENTAL AFFAIRS
INTELLIGENCE

July 29, 1981

Mr. Robert R. Twitchell
5719 Cady Road
Everett, Washington 98203

Dear Bob:

Thank you for your letter of July 15 in further reference to the identification of the bodies recovered at Betio, Tarrawa.

Upon receipt of your letter, I asked officials of the Military Casualty and Memorial Affairs Division again for a status report on my initial inquiry concerning the identification of these remains. They have unofficially informed me that the investigation is not complete as yet. It was indicated that the identification done to this point has not been accepted and it could not be anticipated what the final recommendation would be.

Nevertheless, if I have not received further word by mid September, I will ask the CMA officials for a written update on this matter.

It has indeed been a "hot" summer in D.C. and I am looking forward to my visit to the State.

With best wishes.

Sincerely yours,

Henry M. Jackson, U.S.S.

HMJ:zdb

226

Robert R. Bob Twitchell
5719 Cady Road
Everett, Wa 98203

October 27th 1981

The Honorable Henry M. Jackson
United States Senate
Washington, D.C. 21510

Dear Scoop:

Please forgive my persistance in asking your help to resolve
the case of the (3) United States Marines whose remains were brought
home from Tarawa.

I would be most appreciative to learn the outcome of the
hearing and identification. I am enclosing a copy of your last letter dated July 29th 1981 as reference.

Many thanks for all your kind and welcome assistance.

Sincerely

Robert R. Bob Twitchell

227

JOHN TOWER, TEX., CHAIRMAN

STROM THURMOND, S.C.   JOHN C. STENNIS, MISS.
BARRY GOLDWATER, ARIZ.   HENRY M. JACKSON, WASH.
JOHN W. WARNER, VA.   HOWARD W. CANNON, NEV.
GORDON J. HUMPHREY, N.H.   HARRY F. BYRD, JR., VA.
WILLIAM S. COHEN, MAINE   SAM NUNN, GA.
ROGER W. JEPSEN, IOWA   GARY HART, COLO.
DAN QUAYLE, IND.   J. JAMES EXON, NEBR.
'EMIAH DENTON, ALA.   CARL LEVIN, MICH.

    AHETT B. DAWSON, STAFF DIRECTOR AND CHIEF COUNSEL

United States Senate

COMMITTEE ON ARMED SERVICES
WASHINGTON, D.C. 20510

November 12, 1981

Mr. Robert R. Twitchell
5719 Cady Road
Everett, Washington 98203

Dear Bob:

In reply to your most recent letter concerning the identification of the three Marine bodies discovered on Tarawa, the first week in October I asked for a status report of this case.

This morning an official of the Military Casualty and Memorial Affairs Division telephoned to advise me of the latest information. I am afraid it is not too satisfactory. At this point no definite identification has been made but the report of findings to date is this:

a) One body is unidentifiable due to lack of positive evidence.

b) The remains of the second body will most likely be identified but the conclusions are not definite as yet. Reevaluation of the findings has not been completed.

c) Investigation of the third remains is finished but, because the evidence is inconclusive, CMA is unhappy with the findings and tentatively plans to recommend "unidentifiable."

I have been assured that the case remains open but that when it is completed and a final report is prepared, I will be furnished a copy. It was indicated, however, that this cannot be done until after next-of-kin notification. Because of the great amount of time which has elapsed, finding such relatives could present additional delays.

It appears this case will not be cleared up soon and perhaps it will never be completely resolved. In any event, when I receive further information, I will certainly let you know.

With best regards.

Sincerely yours,

Henry M. Jackson, U.S.S.

HMJ:zdb

228

JOHN TOWER, TEX., CHAIRMAN

STROM THURMOND, S.C. JOHN C. STENNIS, MISS.
BARRY GOLDWATER, ARIZ. HENRY M. JACKSON, WASH.
JOHN W. WARNER, VA. HOWARD W. CANNON, NEV.
GORDON J. HUMPHREY, N.H. HARRY F. BYRD, JR., VA.
WILLIAM S. COHEN, MAINE SAM NUNN, GA.
ROGER W. JEPSEN, IOWA GARY HART, COLO.
DAN QUAYLE, IND.   J. JAMES EXON, NEBR.
'EMIAH DENTON, ALA. CARL LEVIN, MICH.

.HETT B. DAWSON, STAFF DIRECTOR AND CHIEF COUNSEL

𝕌nited 𝕊tates 𝕊enate

COMMITTEE ON ARMED SERVICES
WASHINGTON, D.C. 20510

February 11, 1982

Mr. Robert R. Twitchell
719 Cady Road
Everett, Washington 98203

Dear Bob:

  Today authorities of the Military Casualty and
Memorial Affairs Division telephoned to bring me up-to-
date on identification of the three remains discovered
on Tarawa.

  I am pleased to tell you that identity of one of
the bodies has been established and the next-of-kin
notified. The Marine was PFC Thomas Scurlock; home
of record is Alta Loma, Texas.

  Burial, with full military honors, will be held
in Hawaii with interment in Honolulu National Cemetery.
Determination of the date of the ceremony is the obli-
gation of the family and, as yet, has not been set.

  Casualty officials reconfirmed the information I
related in my letter to you of November 12 concerning
the other two remains; however, they are now reasonably
convinced that one body was not a Marine, but a civilian.
This is not a final conclusion though, and further
investigation is pending. As you know, one of the remains
was determined unidentifiable.

  If investigation reveals new evidence or changes
the information I have received to this point, the
Casualty office has assured me of notification.

  With best wishes.

        Sincerely yours,

        Henry M. Jackson, U.S.S.

HMJ:zdb

229

United States Senate

COMMITTEE ON ARMED SERVICES
WASHINGTON, D.C. 20510

March 16, 1982

Mr. Robert R. Twitchell
5719 Cady Road
Everett, WA 98203

Dear Bob:

    Thank you for your very kind letter of February 19 regarding the identification of the remains found on Tarawa.

    I was very sorry that I was not notified of the date of the burial for PFC Schurlock until after the ceremony had taken place. I was advised that, inasmuch as no next-of-kin were able to attend the service, the family requested it be held at the earliest possible time.

    Without written permission by his sisters -- who are elderly -- military officials could not release much information to me in accordance with the provisions of the Privacy Act. I am certainly sorry that, due to this circumstance, I was not able to make inquiry about space-available travel for you to attend the funeral.

    I was pleased to learn of the publication of your book One Returned. I am glad that I could have been helpful to you in that effort.

    With best wishes.

Sincerely yours,

Henry M. Jackson, U.S.S.

HMJ:zbd

230

Robert R. Bob Twitchell
5719 Cady Road
Everett, Wash. 98203

March 15th 1982

The Honorable Henry M. Jackson
United States Senate
Washington, D.C. 21520

Dear Scoop:

My warmest thanks to you for your kind consideradion this
afternoon, in having your secretary call with the information
in refrence to the services for P.F.C. Thomas Scurlock, in
Hawaii.

I was, and still am extremely dissapointed at not being
able to attend the Military Ceremony, feeling strongly that
someone who shared the horrors of, "Tarawa," with P.F.C. Thomas
Scurlock should have present to mourn, and salute, as the bugline
sounded taps.

I am most appreciative of all you have done, and have told
many of my friends of your tremendous help, but mostly, that you
really care.

You have been so generous but I would request yet another
favor from your office. Would it be possible to get a picture
of the Military Ceremony, if one was held, or in tha absence of
that, a picture of the grave site showing the headstone, along
with the location of the grave in the cemetary.

One day soon, I hope to be able to lay a wreath at the headstone of PFC Scurlocks grave, as I promised her sister I would do
when I talked with her on Sunday February 28th 1982. A much greater honor would be for you to accompany me, and be a part of that
ceremony, as it was only through your dilligence and careing, this
hero, Thomas Scurlock, was returned home to rest on American soil.

Many thanks and best wishes

Robert R. Bob Twitchell

DEPARTMENT OF THE NAVY
HEADQUARTERS UNITED STATES MARINE CORPS
WASHINGTON, D.C. 20380

APR 8 4 31 PM '82

IN REPLY REFER TO
MSPA-1-4-sgh
3040

6 APR 1982

The Honorable Henry M. Jackson
United States Senate
Washington, D.C. 20510

Dear Mr. Jackson:

This is in further response to your inquiries concerning
remains found on Tarawa.

Seventeen remains were identified as portions of ethnic
Japanese. They have been returned to Japan.

A positive identification was made for the remains of Private
First Class Thomas L. SCURLOCK, U. S. Marine Corps. At the
request of his sister, Miss Barbara Scurlock, his remains were
interred in the National Memorial Cemetery of the Pacific,
Honolulu, Hawaii, on February 26, 1982. Full military honors
were provided by Marine Corps personnel.

The information provided above concerns inquiries from your
constituent, Mr. Robert R. "Bob" Twitchell of Everett,
Washington.

Your interest in Marine Corps matters is appreciated and
I trust the foregoing information satisfactorily answers
your inquiry.

                    Sincerely,

                    ROY L. BELLI
               Colonel, U. S. Marine Corps
             Director, Personnel Services Division
        By direction of the Commandant of the Marine Corps;

232

JOHN C. STENNIS, MISS., CHAIRMAN

HENRY M. JACKSON, WASH.   JOHN TOWER, TEX.
HOWARD W. CANNON, NEV.   STROM THURMOND, S.C.
HARRY F. BYRD, JR., VA.   BARRY GOLDWATER, ARIZ.
SAM NUNN, GA.   JOHN W. WARNER, VA.
JOHN C. CULVER, IOWA   GORDON J. HUMPHREY N.H.
GARY HART, COLO.   WILLIAM S. COHEN, MAINE
ROBERT MORGAN, N.C.   ROGER W. JEPSEN, IOWA
*JAMES EXON, NEBR.
  U. LEVIN, MICH.

FRANCIS J. SULLIVAN, STAFF DIRECTOR

United States Senate

COMMITTEE ON ARMED SERVICES
WASHINGTON, D.C. 20510

April 14, 1982

Mr. Robert R. Twitchell
5719 Cady Road
Everett, WA 98203

Dear Bob:

As a follow-up to your telephone conversation with
Mrs. Brighton of my staff, I am enclosing some additional
information regarding the remains found on Tarawa.

Concerning your request for pictures of the internment
cereomonies of Private Scurlock, I have been advised that
all pictures were furnished to his sisters in Texas and
are not available through the Military Casualty and Memorial
Affairs Division. I am very sorry I could not have been more
helpful in obtaining prints of these pictures. Inasmuch as
you have been in contact with Private Scurlock's sisters,
you may wish to contact them direct in this regard.

Additionally, I have attached the policy governing
space-available travel. While I am unaware of your retire-
ment status, Air Force authorities indicated that travel on
military flights can be easily arranged through McChord Air
Force base if you fall under the provisions of eligibility
as listed in the policy.

I surely agree that it would be most appropriate for
you to lay a wreath at Private Scurlock's grave. I hope
you are able to make a trip to Honolulu for this purpose
very soon.

With best wishes.

Sincerely yours,

Henry M. Jackson, U.S.S.

HMJ:zbd

Enc. 1-C Navy letter
     1-C Air Force Policy

233